CASS GILBERT, ARCHITECT

CASS GILBERT · A·N·A·
BY KENYON COX, 1907·

SOURCES OF AMERICAN ARCHITECTURE

CASS GILBERT, ARCHITECT

MODERN TRADITIONALIST

SHARON IRISH

SERIES EDITOR: ROBERT A. M. STERN

THE MONACELLI PRESS

ily,
ffolding of all

First published in the United States of America in 1999 by
The Monacelli Press, Inc.
10 East 92nd Street, New York, New York 10128.

Library of Congress Cataloging-in-Publication Data
Irish, Sharon, date.
Cass Gilbert, architect : modern traditionalist / Sharon Irish.
p.   cm.—(Sources of American architecture)
Includes bibliographical references and index.
ISBN 1-885254-90-3
1. Gilbert, Cass, 1859–1934—Criticism and interpretation.
2. Eclecticism in architecture—United States. I. Gilbert, Cass,
1859–1934. II. Title. III. Series.
NA737.G5I74   1998
720'.92—dc21   98-20358

Printed and bound in Singapore

Designed by Abigail Sturges

*Front cover: Cass Gilbert, F. W. Woolworth Company Building,
New York City, 1910–13. Sketch of entry lobby by Thomas R.
Johnson, April 15, 1912. New-York Historical Society.
(See plate 24.)*

*Back cover: Cass Gilbert, F. W. Woolworth Company Building,
New York City, 1910–13. Study by Thomas R. Johnson,
April 25, 1910. New-York Historical Society. (See plate 23.)*

*Page 1: Cass Gilbert, detail of drawing of many of the large
projects developed during his career, August 1928. Prints and
Photographs Division, Library of Congress. (See fig. 135.)*

*Frontispiece: Kenyon Cox, portrait of Cass Gilbert, 1907,
presented to the National Academy of Design upon Gilbert's
election to membership. National Academy of Design,
New York City.*

CONTENTS

6   AUTHOR'S PREFACE

7   EDITOR'S FOREWORD

COLOR PLATES

12   INTRODUCTION

16   CHAPTER 1
THE EARLY YEARS
Building a Practice in the Midwest

50   CHAPTER 2
THE MOVE TO NEW YORK
"My Ship Really Has Come In"

74   CHAPTER 3
LEADERSHIP IN CIVIC DESIGN
Nationwide Commissions

114   CHAPTER 4
BALANCING ACT
Commercial Heights and Civic Monumentality

164   CONCLUSION

168   ACKNOWLEDGMENTS

170   NOTES

186   SELECTED BUILDINGS

189   READINGS

191   INDEX

AUTHOR'S PREFACE

"Far from implying the repetition of what has been, tradition presupposes the reality of what endures," wrote the composer Igor Stravinsky. "It appears as an heirloom, a heritage that one receives on condition of making it bear fruit before passing it on to one's descendants."[1] The traditions that endured for the architect Cass Gilbert were those of Western Europe from about the twelfth century on, and those of ancient Greece and Rome. He received this heritage gratefully and respectfully, reworked it, and passed it on in his own designs. Most of his buildings achieve excellence—they delight the eye, they serve their purpose, and they are structurally sound—within the confines of traditional styles. In fact, stylistic boundaries may provide some clues to Gilbert's success: without the demands of inventing a new style, the architect was able to explore variations and possibilities within "what endures" to suit himself and his clients.

This book, the first monograph devoted to Gilbert's work, is neither a definitive biography nor a comprehensively illustrated catalog. It is rather an attempt to survey the architecture of Cass Gilbert throughout his fifty-year career and to highlight a few issues that his work raises. A brief bibliography on Gilbert and a selected list of his works can be found on pages 186–90.

— S.I.

EDITOR'S FOREWORD

It is my hope that with the publication of this monograph, Cass Gilbert will once again enjoy the esteem that was his one hundred years ago when he was a leader in American architecture. Gilbert's was an immense talent. An inventor but not an innovator, he worked within the parameters of established architectural modalities, mastering grammar and syntax, as well as vocabularies of details, as few have ever done. Gilbert's work is second to none in its command of composition and vividness of detail.

Until recently Gilbert was neglected by architects and only partially treated by historians. Although some five dissertations, one of which was written by Sharon Irish, the author of this volume in the Sources of American Architecture series, have been devoted to aspects of Gilbert's work, his career as a whole has never received monographic treatment. This kind of neglect did not occur at the time of his early maturity—the 1890s and early 1900s—when the quality and scope of his work were widely appreciated, so much so that he was able to transfer a regional practice in the Midwest to a national one headquartered in New York, a feat then typical in the world of corporations but almost never accomplished in architecture.

Gilbert's early work, though inventive and even searching, reflected prevailing trends. He began with modestly sized houses in the Shingle Style. At the peak of his career he adopted the revived classicism of the American Renaissance, to which he remained loyal to the end, even when challenged by the nascent modernism of the 1920s and early 1930s.

While Gilbert's United States Custom House (1899–1907) is a masterwork of the American Renaissance, an imposing landmark on a key site, his Gothic-inspired Woolworth Company Building (1910–13) showed that he was no ideologue of style: civic buildings were one thing, those dedicated to commerce quite another. The Woolworth Building, Gilbert's best-known building, is unique among the great American corporate buildings in its continuous ability to command the status it enjoyed when it was new. Almost ninety years ago it was designated the "cathedral of commerce," and so it remains, admired by architects and by the public. With his twenty-five-story Federal Courthouse (1929–36) in New York, an incomparable work of cultural and physical contextuality, Gilbert, following the example of Bertram Grosvenor Goodhue's Nebraska State House in Lincoln, Nebraska, synthesized the classicism that best expresses American democracy and the skyscraper form that throughout the twentieth century has represented American enterprise, energy, and modernity.

Gilbert's Supreme Court Building (1928–35) in Washington, D.C., is conventional, but in the best sense of that term. It was the first building purposely built to house the most important court in the United States. Ignoring the stylistic modernism of his day, Gilbert did not even chose a modernizing classicism, preferring to hold true to the classical ideal that governed the nation's first architects. His design embodies the judiciary system in a building that has become one of the country's most revered architectural symbols. Opened at the depth of the Great Depression, when undercurrents of political and social unrest threatened the country's stability, Gilbert's restatement of Jefferson's contention that classical architecture could best establish a convincing setting for the rituals of American democracy rose above stylistic trends that called for new, self-referential building forms.

With Sharon Irish's insightful monograph, I hope the doors of perception, free of any particular aesthetic ideology, will be open to a wide public that will once again admire the achievements of an architect whose steadfast commitment to the ideals of the individual clients and institutions he served has left us with impressive, beautiful, and meaningful works of architecture.

—R.A.M.S.

COLOR PLATES

Union Capitol

St Thomas N.Y.

Durham Cathedral.

St Louis Art Museum.

notre
Dames
de Paris

HOTEL ORMOND
ORMOND BEACH
FLORIDA

1 Parthenon

7 - Bays.

3
} 3 main
2 horizontal
divisions
1

n.y. Custom House

woolworth

Taj Mahal.

San Marco
5 domes

mch 20 1915.

Plate 1 (preceding pages). Cass Gilbert, sketch of world monuments with some of his designs, 1915. Monuments include (left to right, top to bottom): Minnesota State Capitol, St. Paul; Egyptian pyramids and obelisks; Notre Dame Cathedral, Paris; Parthenon, Athens; St. Thomas Episcopal Church, New York City (Cram, Goodhue and Ferguson, 1913); Durham Cathedral, England; Woolworth Building, New York City; United States Custom House, New York City; St. Louis Art Museum, expansion project; Taj Mahal, Agra, India; San Marco, Venice. Cass Gilbert Collection, Prints and Photographs Division, Library of Congress.

Plate 2. Cass Gilbert, Latin Quarter, Paris, France, 1880 (detail). Watercolor and pencil on paper. Bequest of Emily Finch Gilbert through Julia Post Bastedo, executor, National Museum of American Art, Smithsonian Institution.

Plate 3. Cass Gilbert, Latin Quarter, Paris, France, 1880. Watercolor and pencil on paper. Bequest of Emily Finch Gilbert through Julia Post Bastedo, executor, National Museum of American Art, Smithsonian Institution.

Latin Quarter 1880

Gilbert

Plate 4. Cass Gilbert, house on Virginia Avenue [sic, *actually on Ashland Avenue*] *for Elizabeth Wheeler Gilbert (Cass Gilbert's mother), St. Paul, Minnesota, 1882–84. Wash on gray paper. New-York Historical Society.*

Plate 5. Cass Gilbert, William Lightner house, St. Paul, Minnesota, 1893. Perspective drawing. New-York Historical Society.

Elevation on Dayton Ave

Plate 6. Gilbert
and Taylor, Dayton
Avenue Presbyter-
ian Church, St.
Paul, Minnesota,
1886. Elevation
sketch. New-York
Historical Society.

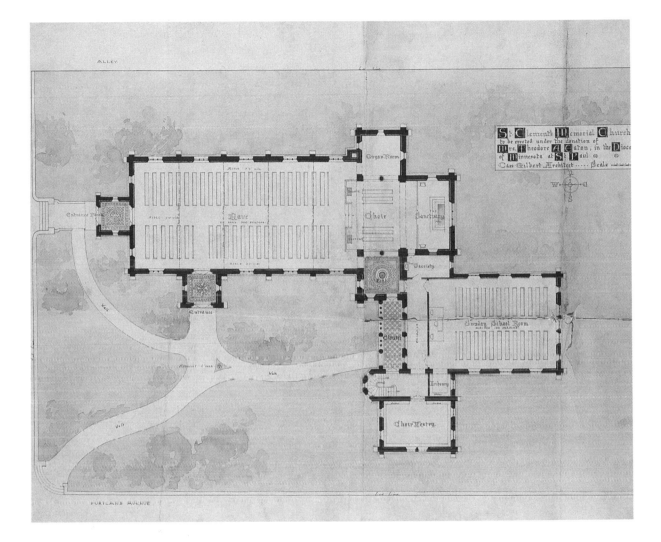

*Plate 7. Cass
Gilbert, St.
Clement's
Episcopal Church,
St. Paul, Minne-
sota, 1894–95.
Original plan.
New-York Histori-
cal Society.*

Plate 8. Cass Gilbert, Broadway Chambers Building, New York City, 1899–1900. Preliminary sketch by Thomas Holyoke, November 3, 1897. New-York Historical Society.

Plate 9. Broadway Chambers Building. Preliminary sketch by "CG," 1897. New-York Historical Society.

Plate 10. Cass Gilbert, United States Custom House, New York City, 1899–1907. Perspective study by William P. Foulds, January 23, 1900. New-York Historical Society.

·V·S· CVSTOM HOVSE, NEW YORK ——— BOWLING GREEN ELEVATION·

Plate 11. United
States Custom
House. Perspective
study by Thomas
R. Johnson, c.1900.
New-York His-
torical Society.

Plate 12. Cass Gilbert, Festival Hall for Louisiana Purchase Exposition, St. Louis, Missouri, 1904. Rendering by Jules Guérin. New-York Historical Society.

Plate 13. Cass Gilbert, watercolor of Baths of Caracalla, Rome, Italy, 1880. Bequest of Emily Finch Gilbert through Julia Post Bastedo, executor, National Museum of American Art, Smithsonian Institution.

·STUDY FOR FINNEY CHAPEL·

Plate 14. Cass Gilbert, Finney Memorial Chapel, Oberlin College, Oberlin, Ohio, 1905–8. Elevation sketch. New-York Historical Society.

Plate 15. Finney Memorial Chapel. Proposed interior decoration, watercolor and gouache over graphite, 1907. Allen Memorial Art Museum, Oberlin, Ohio.

Plate 16. Cass Gilbert, Allen Memorial Art Building, Oberlin College, Oberlin, Ohio, 1914–17. Color pastel of exterior. Cass Gilbert Collection, Prints and Photographs Division, Library of Congress.

Plate 17 (opposite). Cass Gilbert, watercolor of interior of cloister in Monreale, Sicily, 1902. Bequest of Emily Finch Gilbert through Julia Post Bastedo, executor, National Museum of American Art, Smithsonian Institution.

Plate 18. Cass Gilbert, watercolor of Durham Cathedral, England, 1913. Of the cathedral, Gilbert wrote to his wife in 1906: "Old ivory, soft dull gold, low toned lilac and violet are mellowed in the marvellous combinations which time alone can perfect." (Gilbert to Julia Gilbert, August 1, 1906, Cass Gilbert Collection, Manuscripts Division, LofC). Bequest of Emily Finch Gilbert through Julia Post Bastedo, executor, National Museum of American Art, Smithsonian Institution.

*Plate 19. Cass
Gilbert, St. Louis
Public Library,
St. Louis, Missouri,
1907–12. Presenta-
tion drawing by
Birch Burdette
Long, 1912. New-
York Historical
Society.*

*Plate 20. Cass
Gilbert, University
of Texas Library
(now called Battle
Hall), Austin,
Texas, 1909–11.
Elevation drawing,
c.1910. New-York
Historical Society.*

*Plate 21. Cass
Gilbert, James Scott
Memorial Fountain,
Belle Isle, Detroit,
Michigan, 1921–22.
Color rendering
by G.S.K. (G. S.
Keally), December
18, 1919. New-York
Historical Society.*

Plate 22. Cass Gilbert, West Street Building, New York City, 1905–7. Rendering with tower by Birch Burdette Long. New-York Historical Society.

Plate 23. Cass Gilbert, F. W. Woolworth Company Building, New York City, 1910–13. Study by Thomas R. Johnson, April 25, 1910. New-York Historical Society.

Plate 24. F. W. Woolworth Company Building. Sketch of entry lobby by Thomas R. Johnson, April 15, 1912. New-York Historical Society.

Plate 25. Cass Gilbert, Austin, Nichols and Company Warehouse, Brooklyn, New York City, 1909–23. Rendering by Thomas R. Johnson, 1912. New-York Historical Society.

Plate 26. Cass Gilbert, Minnesota State Capitol, St. Paul, Minnesota, 1895–1905. Interior corridor. Copyright 1977, Saari and Forrai, Photography, Minneapolis, Minnesota.

CASS GILBERT, ARCHITECT

INTRODUCTION

The year 1879 was propitious for a young man to begin an architectural career in the United States. Architecture schools in the United States had matured in the decade after the Civil War to the extent that one could obtain adequate professional training without struggling to enter the highly competitive Ecole des Beaux-Arts in Paris.[1] The latter part of the nineteenth century was a generally prosperous time, with highly skilled craftspeople and abundant cheap labor, as well as raw and manufactured goods that could be transported readily by rail or ship, and clients who were looking to invest their wealth in buildings.[2] Enter Cass Gilbert (1859–1934): twenty years old in 1879.[3] He had a strong constitution, artistic talent, business sense, and sheer gumption. He worked relentlessly, he could win commissions, both in competition and by persuasion, he had a good eye for detail and massing, and he could stand his ground against government institutions and countermanding clients. Still, his success as an architect and as a businessman was aided in good measure by a world that wanted what he had to offer.

And offer it he did. Time and again, Gilbert obtained commissions to build some of the major monuments of his generation. The Minnesota State Capitol in St. Paul, the United States Custom House, the Woolworth Company Building, and the New York Life Insurance Company Building in New York City, the United States Military Ocean Terminal in Brooklyn, and the United States Supreme Court Building in Washington, D.C., were designed by his office. He pleased his clients for the most part, and his buildings captured the attention of the likes of Marcel Duchamp, Le Corbusier, and Richard Neutra.[4] Louis Sullivan (1856–1924) was just three years his senior, but died ten years before Gilbert, isolated and poor. Frank Lloyd Wright (1867–1959) was only eight years younger than Gilbert, and grew up in Wisconsin, next door to Gilbert's home state of Minnesota, but was appreciated abroad more than in the United States during the peak of Gilbert's career in the 1910s and 1920s. From our vantage point at the end of the twentieth century, the history of architecture can now accommodate Sullivan, Wright, Gilbert, and many others who approached architectural design in disparate ways.

While a rallying cry in the nineteenth century was to find an architectural style appropriate to the urban industrial era, for Gilbert style was only a means to an end. The desired outcome was not stylistic consistency but a satisfied client and, at the least, a satisfactory building. Thus his adaptations of ancient Greek, Italian Gothic or Renaissance, English medieval, and American Colonial forms for modern-era buildings were not fickle choices but rather derived from the exigencies of each commission.

Gilbert sought counsel in the styles that he had so admired in Europe as well as in the interpretations of them by his American colleagues. In many cases Gilbert's fluency in several stylistic vocabularies allowed him a flexibility that resulted in buildings that looked familiar and conventional but still served modern needs.[5] As will be seen in the coming chapters, Gilbert selected a style to help solve problems he believed were posed by building programs. He made stylistic choices contingent upon the site, the client's needs and wishes, and the building type, guided by precedents. This reliance on tradition served him well throughout his career. One Gilbert sketch of well-known buildings juxtaposed with his own at once pays homage to some of his inspirations and perhaps serves as evidence of what he termed his "audacious egotism"[6] (pl. 1).

While Frank Lloyd Wright turned away from the career path that Chicago architect Daniel Burnham (1846–1912) offered him, Gilbert nearly joined Burnham's firm in 1891.[7] Documents do not clarify why the association between the two men fell through, but it could have been due to a clash of egos. Certainly the two men shared a commitment to large-scale urban design. Where Wright had joined Louis Sullivan in Chicago in 1888, Gilbert eyed the East Coast from the Midwest. He first studied with Eugène Létang at the Massachusetts Institute of Technology (M.I.T.), and, following a sketching tour of Europe, entered the offices of the up-and-coming firm of McKim, Mead and White in 1880.

The usual path taken by a young American interested in architecture in the 1870s lay in an apprenticeship in an architect's office, the larger the better. Very often the youngster would begin as an unpaid errand boy, then work his way up through the drafting room, drawing and studying on his own to improve his skills and expand his portfolio. If time and money permitted, the apprentice would travel in Europe, continuing to study buildings through careful looking and sketching. Upon his return from abroad, the young man might find further work in an architect's office, or start out on his own. The travel sketches and projects on which the apprentice had worked often substantially informed his mature practice, as there was little professional development and only a small body of older buildings in most American cities to guide him.

But the latter decades of the nineteenth century were also years of significant change in the architectural profession. Increasingly those interested in architecture tried to get some formal education in addition to experience in an architect's office. There arose architectural training programs at American universities as well as sketch clubs and professional organizations. Cass Gilbert entered the profession, then, at a turning point in American architecture.

Born in Zanesville, Ohio, on November 29, 1859, Gilbert, the middle of three sons, was named for a distant relative, Lewis Cass.[8] His parents were Elizabeth Fulton Wheeler Gilbert (?–1897) and Samuel Augustus Gilbert (?–1868), whose family had lived in Zanesville for at least two generations.[9] Samuel Gilbert was a surveyor, employed primarily by the United States Coast Survey. In 1927 the portrait painter DeWitt McClellan Lockman (1870–1957) conducted interviews with well-known New Yorkers, and Cass Gilbert was among them.[10] Gilbert related to Lockman his family's departure from Zanesville in 1868. They traveled down the Muskingum River to Marietta, and then boarded a packet boat loaded with glass from Pittsburgh, following the Ohio River to the Mississippi. After two weeks of river travel, the Gilberts arrived in St. Paul, Minnesota. Cass Gilbert and his mother and two brothers remained in St. Paul despite Samuel Gilbert's death just after they arrived. He attended preparatory school in Minneapolis, and in 1876 began architectural training in the St. Paul office of Abraham M. Radcliffe (1827–86).[11] After eighteen months in Radcliffe's office, young Gilbert briefly joined a surveying party in 1878 for the Hudson and River Falls Railroad in Wisconsin.

With his boyhood friends James Knox Taylor (1857–1929?) and Clarence H. Johnston (1859–1936), Gilbert enrolled in the two-year architectural drafting program at the Massachusetts Institute of Technology in 1878.[12] Clarence Johnston stayed at M.I.T. only a few months; Gilbert himself left after the first year.[13] The design program was run by the Beaux-Arts-trained architect Eugène Létang, who had been hired by William Robert Ware in 1872.[14] On the French Beaux-Arts method, Gilbert commented: "I believe heartily in the general training of the Ecole des Beaux-arts which Mr. Letang so admirably represented, but I think the training that is desirable for France is not always usable in America."[15] The young man from Minnesota polished his drawing and design skills sufficiently at M.I.T. to win first prize in 1879 from the Boston Society of Architects for his "Billiard Hall and Casino," and second prize for his portfolio of drawings; he also received first mention for a Pompeiian restoration.[16]

Following his studies at M.I.T., Gilbert worked for the United States Coast and Geodetic Survey as an assistant surveyor to earn money for travel. Early in 1880, he used his savings, along with funds from his father's estate and his grandmother to travel in France, Italy, and England for several months[17] (pls. 2 and 3). Thus began his lifelong practice of watercolor sketching, filling notebooks with building profiles and details, vistas of villages and country-

side, and occasional figures. These notebooks became reference works for
Gilbert for the rest of his career. In them, he could find profiles of moldings,
exact measurements, and silhouettes of architecture that he studied in
repeated trips to Europe. During his first trip to Europe, Gilbert had hoped
to find employment in an architect's office in London but was unable to do
so.[18] He then returned to New York City short of funds and started to work in
the office of McKim, Mead and White in September 1880, helping with the
firm's residential projects. He supervised construction of the Ross Winans
House (1882–83) in Baltimore, for example.[19] Gilbert reminisced at the end
of his career that

> there must be a spirit in the offices as well as an esprit du [sic] corps. When
> I was a draftsman there were certain offices I wouldn't have gone into, at
> any salary. For instance I preferred to stay with McKim, Mead and White at
> $20 a week than go to Herter Brothers or Burnham and Root's for $60 and
> I had those offers from both.[20]

Like many young men with talent and ambition, Gilbert honed his design skills
in the growing firm and then struck out on his own. In August of 1882, he
wrote to Johnston: "I have been so long at McKim's and have in a certain way
'ran the scale' in that office that I feel it is getting time for me to get out of it
unless I have a certainty of something more than a draughtsman's position."[21]
Wanting to be closer to his family (his mother's health was poor), Gilbert
returned to St. Paul in December of 1882 as McKim, Mead and White's repre-
sentative in the West (that is, between Minnesota and Washington State).
He was charged with overseeing the construction of terminals, hotels, railroad
depots, and offices for the Northern Pacific Railroad, then controlled by Henry
Villard.[22] Fortunately for Gilbert, he had begun to obtain other jobs, because
the NPRR was reeling financially at the time, and Villard's finances would
finally collapse in 1884. The ambitious goal of a Midwestern office of McKim,
Mead and White, with Gilbert at its head, was not met. Still, the attempt got
Gilbert back to Minnesota, introduced him to some key people, and set him
on the course he would follow for the next fifteen years.

THE EARLY YEARS

Building a Practice in the Midwest

B y 1885, Gilbert formed a partnership in St. Paul with James Knox Taylor, his friend and former classmate in both Minneapolis and Massachusetts.[1] The two young architects began their practice in a thriving area.[2] Gilbert apparently felt that Taylor would complement his own talents. To a draftsman in McKim, Mead and White's office, Edward Spiers, he wrote that Taylor was expert in "matters of contracts, superintendence, and general conduct of affairs."[3] While Gilbert's signature is on many renderings published by the firm, it is hard to know what each partner contributed. Gilbert and Taylor worked together until 1891. Taylor moved to Philadelphia in 1892.[4]

The architect John Root (of Burnham and Root) explained the intense rivalry between Minneapolis and St. Paul in 1890:

> In cases like St. Paul and Minneapolis, every move of either city is watched by the other with the keenest interest, and every structure of importance in one city becomes only the standard to be passed by the other; not only is it their ambition to excel in matters of population and wealth but also in the splendor and prominence of the architectural movement.[5]

Given this competition, the fledgling firm of Gilbert and Taylor had to develop strategies that would give them an edge. Taylor's father, H. Knox Taylor, had a variety of connections useful to them because he was prominent in real estate and a lay leader in the Presbyterian Church.[6] Of course, Gilbert too had contacts among the railroad leaders because of his work for Villard on behalf of McKim, Mead and White. Contacts in clubs and railroad and real-estate companies were a good beginning.[7] Gilbert also married well. On November 29, 1887 (his twenty-eighth birthday), he wed Julia Tappen Finch in Milwaukee. Julia Finch (1862?–1952) was the daughter of a wealthy and prominent attorney, Henry Martyn Finch (1829–84); she brought her own ambition and business sense into Gilbert's life.[8]

*1. Gilbert and
Taylor, Paul
Gotzian house,
St. Paul, Minne-
sota, 1889. Min-
nesota Historical
Society.*

Gilbert knew that connections were crucial to securing commissions. He was one of the founders of the Minnesota Club in 1884—to share "literary and social culture" in St. Paul. James J. Hill (1838–1916), an increasingly powerful figure on the local scene as an executive of what was to become the Great Northern Railroad, was one of the original members of the governing board.[9] Gilbert and his attorney, George Squires (1852–1905), also belonged to the Town and Country Club, a St. Paul golfing club organized in 1888.[10] In 1894 Gilbert was elected president of the Minnesota Chapter of the American Institute of Architects, which had been founded two years earlier.[11]

The challenge for any architect was to make his connections bring in work. While the city of St. Paul was growing rapidly, Gilbert and Taylor had to compete for building commissions not only with other architects but with builders and engineers. Professional architects were a rather new breed, and clients did not necessarily distinguish among these groups. For the public they hoped to serve, then, architects began to define professional boundaries and codify ethics in order to differentiate their services from those of a builder, for example. Gilbert and Taylor and their colleagues had to prove the worth of the well-conceived plans and up-to-date styles they had worked hard to learn. On the one hand, the partners set a standard for quality design in the commissions they did receive; on the other hand, they joined with their colleagues to push for standardized and higher fees, clear contractual agreements, and other, related guidelines.

In their own state, Minnesota architects like Gilbert and Taylor found themselves in competition with East Coast architects. For example, James J. Hill hired the Boston firm of Peabody, Stearns and Furber in 1887 to design his mansion on Summit Avenue in St. Paul. Gilbert was only hired to design the power house, the fence, and the gates.[12]

Because many large business firms, like railroad companies, had their own in-house builders, and because government jobs often were awarded to a designer for political reasons, firms like Gilbert and Taylor had to establish and maintain their niches in private residential, ecclesiastical, and commercial work.[13] During the 1880s, Gilbert and Taylor designed city houses, summer residences, and small office buildings for many members of the clubs they had joined.[14]

In his first twenty years of practice, Gilbert (with or without Taylor) designed about fifty houses. None was remarkable in plan or elevation. What distinguished them are the materials Gilbert chose, the details that made each one unique, and some of their marvelous sites. Because of the appeal of their sites and the livability of these houses, many of them survive, albeit considerably altered. Gilbert's typical scheme was essentially cubic, with the box of the house textured and detailed differently for each client. Sometimes Gilbert

*2. Cass Gilbert,
Gotzian Warehouse
and Wholesale
Shoe Store, St. Paul,
Minnesota, 1895.
Minnesota Historical Society.*

would take an informal turn and ramble beyond the confines of a boxy plan; other times the cubic form would be tightly contained on the site.

Gilbert had already designed a house for his mother, Elizabeth Wheeler Gilbert, in St. Paul in 1882, while he was still in McKim, Mead and White's office (pl. 4). Completed by 1884, the house, still standing at 471 Ashland Avenue in St. Paul, is now quite different from the sketch, which shows a Shingle Style, clapboard structure with projecting gables and many-paned windows that pushed out from a central box. The fenestration, small balconies, and porches were derived from East Coast and English prototypes, like those published in periodicals in the 1870s.[15] The Paul Gotzian house (1889), by contrast, was an unapologetic box of buff limestone (fig. 1). Sited on steep Summit Hill, the Gotzian house itself is cliff-like in its reliance on stone with the roofs of the house and porch serving as ledges. A third-story gable with lacy wooden ornament interrupts the horizontality of the house but effectively marks the central axis. Squat porch columns with foliate capitals resemble the French medieval versions Gilbert recorded in his sketchbook in 1880 while traveling.

A satisfied client often will hire the same firm again, and, in Gilbert's case, this rule built his practice. For example, he was hired to design the Gotzian Warehouse and Wholesale Shoe Store in 1895, after Taylor had departed (fig. 2). Derived from round-arched commercial buildings like the much-published

3. Gilbert and Taylor, Bookstaver Row Houses (also known as Portland Terrace), St. Paul, Minnesota, 1888. E. D. Becker, Minnesota Historical Society.

R. H. White Warehouse Store (1882–83) in Boston by Peabody and Stearns, the Gotzian building's beveled corner bay is flanked by five more bays to each side.[16] Horizontal string courses separate the arched windows from the rectangular openings on the ground and top floors. As exemplified by his work for Gotzian, Gilbert had synthesized medieval, Renaissance, and contemporary vocabularies by the mid-1890s in order to provide his clients with up-to-date buildings characterized by traditional stylistic features. Of this sort of eclectic facility, architect Thomas Tallmadge remarked: "With so many songs at one's command it is too much to expect that the singer will stick to one tune."[17]

Not that Gilbert's designs were willfully capricious. Rather, he adapted different schemes, different motifs for different sites and purposes. Gilbert and Taylor's three-story Bookstaver Row Houses of 1888 in St. Paul, also known as Portland Terrace, recall buildings in Boston's Back Bay (which was rapidly being filled in with brick and stone row houses in the late nineteenth century)[18] (fig. 3). The firm's modest design is distinctive due to the zipperlike effect of projecting bricks at the corners, the oriel windows, and an entry porch on the Kent Street side with stairs tucked under a round arch.[19] Gilbert and Taylor would have known Boston examples from their stay in Massachusetts during 1878–79, as well as from published illustrations of contemporary American and European architecture in the Boston-based *American Architect and Building News.*[20]

While most of the Midwest was under the sway of "medievalism," particularly that derived from the work of Henry Hobson Richardson, Cass Gilbert had returned to St. Paul from the East "with Richardson's medieval imagery in one pocket and McKim, Mead and White's Renaissance Revival in the other."[21] Gilbert's houses usually were inspired by either the American Colonial vernacular, as in the Elizabeth Wheeler Gilbert house, or the Romanesque Revival, as with the Paul Gotzian house, but in St. Paul between 1887 and 1889 Gilbert and Taylor designed the Charles P. Noyes house, which echoed McKim, Mead and White's newly emerging classicism, drawn from eighteenth-century American Georgian and Federal period architecture (fig. 4). McKim, Mead and White's H. A. C. Taylor house in Newport, Rhode Island (1885–86), for example, was a cubical, hipped-roof dwelling with a service wing (fig. 5). Balustraded porches flanked a large arched window that lit the interior stair hall. Another porch, situated at right angles to the other two, projected beyond the parlor and was balanced by a Palladian window. These eighteenth-century motifs reappeared on a smaller scale and in a

4. Gilbert and Taylor, Charles P. Noyes house, St. Paul, Minnesota, 1887–89. Minnesota Historical Society.

5. McKim, Mead and White, H. A. C. Taylor house, Newport, Rhode Island, 1885–86. George Sheldon, Artistic Country Seats.

6. Cass Gilbert, William Lightner house, St. Paul, Minnesota, 1893. Exterior. Tom Lutz, Minnesota Historical Society.

7. Henry Hobson Richardson, J. J. Glessner house, Chicago, Illinois, 1885–87. Glessner House Museum, Chicago, Illinois.

revised configuration on Gilbert and Taylor's Noyes house. Patricia Murphy claims that it "was one of the first Colonial Revival houses to be constructed in the Twin Cities and marked the beginning of the style in the area."[22]

Practicing alone after 1891, Gilbert designed a house in St. Paul for William Lightner in 1893 (fig. 6). Initially he intended to build a Georgian Revival house with corner pilasters and a colonnaded, semicircular porch (pl. 5). The final version of the house retained the Georgian symmetry, but the red and brown sandstone used to mark the entry arch recalls the variegated, rough-hewn stonework characteristic of Richardson. The massing of the Lightner house seems to have been borrowed from Richardson's own Glessner house (1885–87; fig. 7) in Chicago, changed slightly and installed on St. Paul's Summit Avenue. Reduced in size to a cube, the Lightner house paid tribute to the massive facade, arched door, and stubby columns of the Glessner house. Gilbert made minor changes in details, adding a column to Richardson's three on the Glessner house, for example, to separate the central second-story windows and simplifying the windows of the Lightner house to fit under the hipped roof.

While the firm designed many city houses for business associates, Gilbert and Taylor also designed summer homes, accessible by rail in towns just north of St. Paul or west of Minneapolis. A cottage for A. Kirby Barnum (1884) in Dellwood in White Bear Lake, north of St. Paul, drew on Shingle Style residential designs in which a large gable was the dominant motif (fig. 8). Porches for the enjoyment of lake breezes and views opened up the first

8. *Gilbert and Taylor, A. Kirby Barnum cottage, Dellwood, White Bear Lake, Minnesota, 1884.* American Architect and Building News.

9. *William Ralph Emerson, Hemenway house, Manchester-by-the-Sea, Massachusetts, 1883. George Sheldon,* Artistic Country Seats.

floor and made the house seem informally asymmetrical, while in fact the large sitting room was balanced by the dining room across the main hall and the stairs were matched by a vestibule and closet space. Set on a rise near a lake, the natural textures of the materials—stone, wood, and brick— enhanced the retreat-like atmosphere of the cottage. A larger house by an architect Gilbert admired can be compared to this one: William Ralph Emerson's Hemenway house (1883) in Manchester-by-the-Sea, Massachusetts, had a large gable that framed the upper stories and an exterior ground-floor wall

of rough stone[23] (fig. 9). While different in plan, the Hemenway house had stairs tucked away as well. Gilbert and Taylor's Walter S. Morton cottage (c.1891), also in White Bear Lake, had a sheltered porch on three sides (fig. 10). Most of the rooms were lifted up into the shingled two stories above, under a gambrel roof. The effect of a roof floating over outdoor spaces was also seen in Bruce Price's William Kent house (1885) on Tower Hill at Tuxedo Park, New York (fig. 11). Price's Kent house had a cross-shaped plan, and the ground-floor spaces balanced one another around a central stair. Taylor

12. Gilbert and Taylor, J. B. Tarbox cottage, White Bear Lake, Minnesota, 1889–91. Photograph c.1891. Northwest Builder and Decorator, *Minnesota Historical Society.*

13. McKim, Mead and White, Victor Newcomb house, Elberon, New Jersey, 1880–81. George Sheldon, Artistic Country Seats.

14. Cass Gilbert, J. B. Tarbox cottage. Ink and wash on board. New-York Historical Society.

had worked for Bruce Price in the early 1880s, but Price's work also was known from widely available periodicals.

Gilbert and Taylor's Shingle Style houses do not ramble in the way that larger country houses in the East do: their modest size encouraged a tighter plan. Gilbert paid homage to his mentors, McKim, Mead and White, in his J. B. Tarbox cottage of 1889–91, also in White Bear Lake (fig. 12). As Murphy points out, the Tarbox cottage shared a massing scheme with McKim, Mead and White's Victor Newcomb house (1880–81) in Elberon, New Jersey[24] (fig. 13). Low porches broke up the horizontal mass, but, as is evident in Gilbert's pen-and-ink sketch, the Tarbox cottage was simpler (fig. 14).

Two church commissions came by 1886: the Dayton Avenue Presbyterian Church and the Swedenborgian Virginia Street Church, both in St. Paul. The Gilberts attended the Dayton Avenue Church. For this congregation, Gilbert and Taylor provided one space large enough to seat 850 people beneath the dominant gabled roof[25] (fig. 15). The small entry porch stands in contrast to the mass of the church tower and the volume of the sanctuary enclosed by the ridge roof. A second entry is located in the cross gable at the opposite end of the church. Three narrow, round-arched windows step up and down again in both gables. The Dayton Avenue Church plan is indebted to an early Richardson design, the Church of the Unity (1866–69),

in Springfield, Massachusetts. Both architects situated the entrance at the junction of tower and gabled sanctuary. In addition, Gilbert and Taylor's tower for the Dayton Avenue Church, a square block surmounted by a steeple, is similar to Richardson's North Congregational Church (1872–73), also in Springfield. The Dayton Avenue Church, unlike Richardson's Church of the Unity and North Congregational Church, has eyebrow dormers in the roof, a shingled steeple and discrete pinnacles, and windows in round arches. An earlier scheme had a more complicated plan and featured a rose window (pl. 6). The Dayton Avenue Church is built of a dark red Bayfield stone, not unlike the Longmeadow stone that Richardson favored. Montgomery Schuyler believed the Dayton Avenue Church to be "a studied and scholarly performance," even though the tower scheme was "not rhythmic or felicitous."[26]

Not far from the prominent site of the Dayton Avenue Church in St. Paul, Gilbert and Taylor built a small Swedenborgian church on Virginia Street in the Shingle Style (fig. 16). Swedenborgian Christians have a liturgy similar to that of the Lutherans but tenets resembling those of Unitarians. Their sect is small, though it flourished in the late nineteenth century.[27] Gilbert and Taylor's design is domestic in its scale. Indeed, the foundation of river boulders, the clapboard and shingle siding, and the delicate porches all contribute to its success as an intimate house of worship, while the louvered belfry and

15 (opposite). Gilbert and Taylor, Dayton Avenue Presbyterian Church, St. Paul, Minnesota, 1886. The photograph is from the William G. Purcell Papers. Penciled on the photograph is: "Remarkably beautiful stone masonry. They had stone cutters and stone masons who really were artists." Courtesy Northwest Architectural Archives, University of Minnesota Libraries, St. Paul, Minnesota.

16. Gilbert and Taylor, Virginia Street (Swedenborgian) Church, St. Paul, Minnesota, 1886. Minnesota Historical Society.

17. Gilbert and Taylor, German Bethlehem Presbyterian Church, St. Paul, Minnesota, 1890. View from the east. Northwest Builder and Decorator, *courtesy Northwest Architectural Archives, University of Minnesota Libraries, St. Paul, Minnesota.*

spire and a small cross at the gable's peak mark the Virginia Street structure as a religious building. The congregation felt that the large stones represented "fixed truths that will not change."[28] The sanctuary is legible in the long ridge roof. The interior is spare, surmounted by a barrel-vaulted ceiling with exposed timbers. An addition at the east end was designed by Clarence Johnston in 1922.

While it cannot be said that Gilbert and Taylor were innovators in the design of religious buildings, they demonstrated with these two early churches that they could produce pleasing, well-executed buildings for different denominations and congregations. Gilbert clearly had a talent for working up a design for a small church or house, with or without James Taylor. For example, the German Bethlehem Presbyterian Church (1890), lodged at the foot of Ramsey Hill in St. Paul, recalls medieval Europe in its gable front with barge boards curved to look like crucks, a timbered porch, and a corner tower with a broach spire[29] (figs. 17 and 18). The small church was designed for a German-speaking congregation, with two Swiss-born brothers spearheading the effort and apparently suggesting to Gilbert and Taylor some Swiss motifs. Visitors simultaneously climb the hill and the stairs to enter the limestone church. Behind the vestibule in the tower is a small octagonal study. This church design remained one of Gilbert's favorites: he sketched its picturesque profile from memory in 1922.[30]

18. German Bethlehem Presbyterian Church. View from the foot of Summit Hill. Minnesota Historical Society.

Gilbert alone composed St. Clement's Episcopal Church in St. Paul (1894–95) on a much more generous site than that of the German Bethlehem Presbyterian Church (fig. 19). Set back from Portland Avenue, St. Clement's is a retreat reachable by a curved walk through the yard. A lych gate provided access to the property.[31] Initially, the large scheme included a parish hall at right angles to the sanctuary (pl. 7). In his travels, Gilbert had sketched English Gothic parish churches extensively and had admired the Gothic Revival churches of English architects. During his student days, he had written to Clarence Johnston about George Edmund Street, a London-based architect known for his Victorian Gothic churches: "[His] endeavor after *pure Gothic* and his surprising exactness of detail in all his office work have an attraction for me that even the romantic spell of Norman Shaw cannot overcome."[32]

When Mrs. Theodore Eaton, the widow of the rector of St. Clement's Church in New York, donated $25,000 to build a church in Minnesota in her husband's memory, the diocese selected a congregation that had just formed. Gilbert bestowed tradition upon this new group by providing them with a very English-looking parish church of Minnesota limestone.[33] The interior features an exposed hammerbeam ceiling; stencils on the chancel arch and window reveals; and, originally, an encaustic tile floor (fig. 20). Gilbert designed the oak rood screen; the altar and baptismal font are

19. Cass Gilbert, St. Clement's Episcopal Church, St. Paul, Minnesota, 1894–95. Buckbee Mears, Minnesota Historical Society.

20. St. Clement's Episcopal Church. Interior. Clifford Renshaw, Minnesota Historical Society.

21. Cass Gilbert, St. John the Divine Episcopal Church, Moorhead, Minnesota, 1898–99. J. Ferguson, Minnesota Historical Society.

replicas of those in St. Clement's in New York. Gilbert's friend and colleague Clarence Johnston designed the parish hall and narthex in 1913.[34]

The design of St. John the Divine Episcopal Church (1898–99) in Moorhead, Minnesota, represents a variation on ideas given form at the start of Gilbert's career. The Church blends the gable composition of the Dayton Avenue Presbyterian Church with the steep spire, shingles, and boulders of the Virginia Street Church (both from 1886) and creates an impressive composition (fig. 21). It perhaps works because of the odd juxtaposition of the oversized tower and the sanctuary. Gilbert detailed the building well, as can be seen in the eyebrow dormers with carved barge boards that poke out of the roof and an octagonal brick chimney.

Gilbert's partnership with James Taylor had ended in 1891. Just as the firm of Gilbert and Taylor had achieved moderate success with religious and domestic commissions, so did Gilbert continue his solo practice with similar commissions. Another small-scale building type that he explored in the 1890s was the railroad depot. He was able to develop his ideas about the depot over the next two decades in response to the rapid growth of inter- and intraurban transportation systems. In Minnesota, Gilbert designed Great Northern Railroad depots in Anoka (fig. 22) and Willmar (fig. 23), among others, both dated 1891. At the end of the decade, he provided the Great Northern Rail-

34

22. Cass Gilbert, Great Northern Depot, Anoka, Minnesota, 1891. Track-front elevation, ink on linen, drawn by John R. Rachac Jr., August 17–20, 1891. New-York Historical Society.

23. Cass Gilbert, Great Northern Depot (demolished), Willmar, Minnesota, 1891. Street elevation, ink on linen, drawn by John R. Rachac Jr., August 25, 1891. New-York Historical Society.

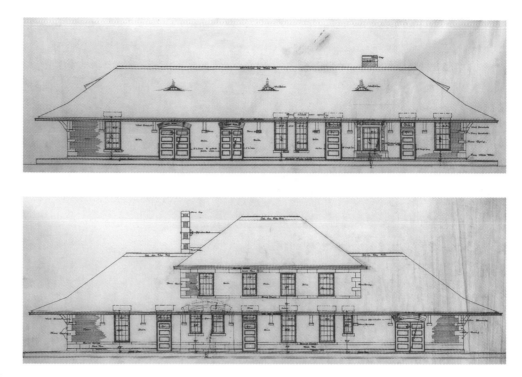

road with a depot at Little Falls, Minnesota (1899). With the exception of some tombs, memorial monuments, and a few more railroad depots, Gilbert stopped designing on a small scale after 1900.[35] A shift toward larger-scale work began with Gilbert and Taylor's commission in 1889 for the Endicott Building in downtown St. Paul, the completion of which also marked the end of their joint practice[36] (figs. 24 and 25).

The development of the Endicott Building (1889–91) was the result of a common phenomenon in the Midwest in the late nineteenth century. Eastern businessmen purchased sites in rapidly growing Western cities as real-estate investments.[37] The two Endicott brothers, Henry and William Jr., of Boston, Massachusetts, had a family dry goods business that supplied Boston as well as markets in Western cities.[38] Gilbert and Taylor designed warehouses and office space for them, with the Endicott Building being the most prominent.[39]

The Endicott Building comprises six stories of offices and shops on an L-shaped lot in downtown St. Paul.[40] Due to its odd site and the severity of the Minnesota winter, the Endicott has a remarkable interior arcade that connects the two parts of the building. From either Fourth Street or Robert Street, the visitor can enter a shop-lined corridor, originally distinguished by a barrel vault of colored glass[41] (fig. 26). Since the Endicott site wrapped around the twelve-story Pioneer Building on the corner, it offered Gilbert and Taylor the opportunity to design two facades.[42] Both facades—of granite, sandstone, and pressed brick—display Renaissance motifs popularized by McKim, Mead and White in the early 1880s. In a penciled annotation to an article about his work,

24. Gilbert and Taylor, Endicott Building, St. Paul, Minnesota, 1889–91. Fourth Street facade. Minnesota Historical Society.

Gilbert noted that the "Villard House influenced me on Endicott."[43] The Villard houses (1881–82) in Manhattan had been on the drawing boards of McKim, Mead and White while Gilbert was still working in their New York office and Joseph Morrill Wells (1853–90), a senior member of the firm, was the architect in McKim, Mead and White's office credited with the Villard design.[44]

Wells's Russell and Erwin Building (1883–84; often called the RussWin Hotel; fig. 27) in New Britain, Connecticut, also seems to have influenced Gilbert and Taylor's Endicott facade organization.[45] Like the RussWin, the Endicott features Renaissance motifs without specific prototypes. Both buildings have stone bases and both are topped by stories in brick and terra cotta separated by secondary cornices. Gilbert sent photographs of the Endicott Building's facades to Wells, who replied in 1889: "The general effect is *very good*, and dignified—and I congratulate you on it."[46]

Fifteenth-century *palazzi* and American adaptations of Italian Renaissance schemes inspired Gilbert and Taylor's designs for the Endicott Building.

27. McKim, Mead and White (Joseph Morrill Wells, designer), Russell and Erwin Building (RussWin Hotel), 1883–84, New Britain, Connecticut. New-York Historical Society.

28. Cass Gilbert, Minnesota State Capitol, St. Paul, Minnesota, 1895–1905. Tracing of competition entry, south front. Minnesota Historical Society.

29. Minnesota State Capitol. South facade. Minnesota Historical Society.

So, too, did Renaissance buildings and American versions thereof provide models for Gilbert when he competed for the commission to design the Minnesota State Capitol (1895–1905).[47] An 1896 tracing shows a dome reminiscent of the sixteenth-century new St. Peter's in Rome, for example (fig. 28). The Board of State Capitol Commissioners agreed with Gilbert's choices of precedents and selected his design (fig. 29). Throughout the ten years that Gilbert was involved with the capitol design and construction his letters and diaries were filled with notes and sketches that reveal his working methods. For example, in 1898 he wrote to a staff member, "I am going to climb the dome of the Florence Cathedral today to make notes of its construction with a view to our work . . . This trip is a very valuable one for the Capitol work as I am constantly finding practical points."[48]

While Gilbert had indeed traveled extensively in Europe to collect ideas, a number of his sources lay closer to home. In 1891 McKim, Mead and White won the competition for the Rhode Island State Capitol (1895–1905; fig. 30). The Minnesota State Capitol Commissioners apparently viewed the Rhode Island scheme as ideal.[49] While the dome designs differ—Rhode

DESIGN FOR MINNESOTA STATE CAPITOL
· ELEVATION OF SOUTH FRONT ·

SCALE ¼ INCH = 1 FOOT

Island's is derived from the English Renaissance work of Sir Christopher Wren—both capitol schemes eschew a pedimented temple front. Both Gilbert and McKim, Mead and White devised plans with the senate and house chambers on the second floor, but Gilbert turned his house wing at right angles to that of the senate.[50] Whereas Gilbert chose to keep the rotunda free as a gathering space, McKim, Mead and White located the main stairway there (figs. 31 and 32).

The 142-foot-high dome interior can be viewed easily from the capitol's rotunda[51] (fig. 33). Because Gilbert kept his rotunda unimpeded, the North Star of brass and thick opalescent glass, lit from the crypt below, captures the eye as visitors pass through the space to the main stairs (figs. 34 and 35). For more efficient vertical circulation, visitors could avoid the grand stair-case and opt for the cantilevered stairs just south of the house chamber (fig. 36). Set in an oval, the stairs curve out from a wall that also provides an inset marble rail. Gilbert would revisit cantilevered staircases at the end of his career with the United States Supreme Court building (fig. 132).

Both the exterior sculpture, particularly the gilded quadriga by Daniel Chester French, and the interior decorations of the Minnesota State Capitol make it a prime example of the collaborative work executed during the American Renaissance, usually dated between 1890 and 1915.[52] Gilbert

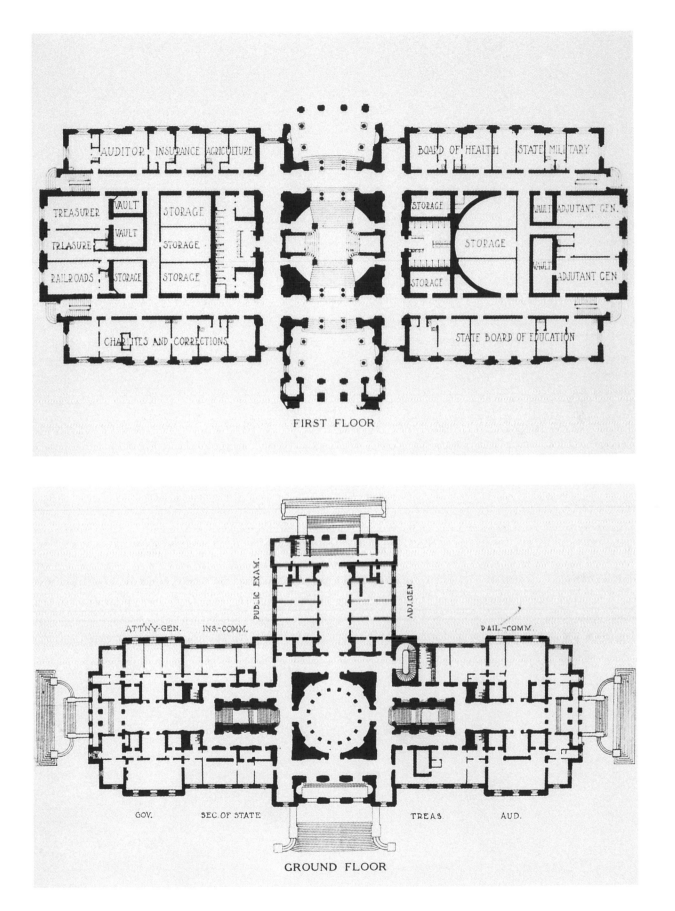

FIRST FLOOR

GROUND FLOOR

33. Minnesota State Capitol. View into dome. C. W. Jerome, Minnesota Historical Society.

34. Minnesota State Capitol. Crypt under rotunda. Edmund A. Brush, Minnesota Historical Society.

35. Minnesota State Capitol. View down main stair toward rotunda. Graphic Arts Studios, Minnesota Historical Society.

pressed hard for allocations to enhance his marble monument, and, when he had succeeded in obtaining the funds, he imported artists from the East Coast. A life-long watercolorist himself, Gilbert conceived of his capitol interior as a three-dimensional color masterpiece, using a wide variety of materials.[53] Gold-hued marbles stand out against Pompeiian red walls (pl. 26). Strongly veined marble columns stimulate the eye from a landing at the top of the stairs. A red-tinted stone frieze complements polished red marble columns with gilded Corinthian capitals. Add to this the stenciled vaults, mural panels, and bronze and brass ornaments and lighting fixtures, and the sum is a rich tribute to Minnesota.[54]

Ironically Gilbert's success with the state capitol commission contributed to the decline of his Minnesota practice in the late 1890s. His insistence on the use of Georgian marble for the exterior made him enemies among local quarriers and railroad men. These Minnesota businessmen had lobbied for the exclusive use of Minnesota stone for the construction of the capitol. When a compromise was reached after considerable controversy, Minnesota granite and sandstone were used for foundation piers, dome supports, foundation walls, and exterior steps, and extensively on the interior, but the marble for the exterior was still imported from Georgia. Gilbert had won that battle, but subsequently complained to his former

36. Minnesota
State Capitol.
Cantilevered stairs.
Stan Waldhauser,
Minnesota Histori-
cal Society.

partner that "My refusal to accede to the demands of politicians and influ-
ential quarrymen and railroad magnates in letting the contract for the
Minnesota State Capitol has . . . almost wipe[d] out my private business
during the last year."[55] During the first decade of the twentieth century,
Gilbert kept an office in St. Paul, but he and his family moved to New York
City in 1899, shortly after he was awarded two large commissions for buildings in Manhattan.

Part of Gilbert's legacy in Minnesota was the training he provided for young
men, some of whom gathered around him in his St. Paul office for a photograph (fig. 37). Thomas Holyoke (1866–1925), who traveled and studied in
Europe in 1890 and 1891 with Gilbert's assistance, worked in the office
from 1889 and continued to oversee the practice in St. Paul until it closed
in 1909, even though he had opened his own practice in 1900.[56] Similarly,
Samuel-Stevens Haskell (1871–1913) was a local boy who joined Gilbert's
office, probably in the late 1880s, and then attended M.I.T. from 1890 to
1891. He found work on the East Coast until 1894, when he registered at
the Ecole des Beaux-Arts in Paris and entered the atelier of Jules-Alexis
Godefroy and Jacques-Eugène Freynet. Haskell was admitted to the first
class of the Ecole in 1896 and remained in France until 1899. On his
return, he entered Gilbert's office in New York and remained until 1903,
when he left with a loan from Gilbert to start his own practice in Montreal
with John Omer Marchand (1872–1936).[57] John R. Rachac Jr. (1873?–1951)
was part of this early trio of associates. Rachac (who changed his name to
Rockart in 1902) entered Gilbert's employ in 1891 and left for Europe in
1899. In 1901 he was admitted to the Ecole des Beaux-Arts and studied at
the atelier of Victor Laloux. That May, Rachac borrowed money from
Gilbert, presumably to travel, and then returned to Gilbert's office in
October of 1902. He worked for Gilbert until the latter's death.[58]

While Gilbert and many of his staff had doubts about the efficacy of French
design methods for American needs, Gilbert clearly supported his employees in their efforts to acquire the coveted French academic training. As a
result of the thorough exposure to architectural precedents that many of
Gilbert's employees had received in Paris, his office staff shared assump-
tions and knowledge that eased the difficulties inherent in teamwork.
Writing to a colleague in 1909, Gilbert explained, "I believe that in our
public buildings where the problems are not dissimilar to those of former
times we may well study the serious and noble proportions of the old buildings and develop along the lines of precedent without interjecting the
extremely modern and utilitarian features of our commercial structures."[59]
With the exception of the United States Military Ocean Terminal (1918–19)
in Brooklyn, none of Gilbert's buildings, commercial or otherwise, can be
described as "extremely modern." The variations on precedents seen in
the Endicott Building and the Minnesota State Capitol would typify
Gilbert's designs throughout his career.

37. Cass Gilbert and his employees in St. Paul during Minnesota Capitol construction. Gilbert is seated on a stool at the front. Minnesota Historical Society.

THE MOVE TO NEW YORK

"My Ship Really Has Come In"

A s a designer clearly challenged by large-scale urban projects, Gilbert had opportunities throughout his career to address the problems of the tall office building at the same time that he created grand civic monuments. In Minnesota, for example, the Endicott Building served as both prelude and counterpoint to Gilbert's work on the state capitol. Gilbert's early work in New York City is balanced by the eighteen-story Broadway Chambers Building (1899–1900), on the one hand, and the monumental U.S. Custom House (1899–1907), on the other. This pair of built projects, and several smaller, related projects, contribute to one theme, that of the appropriate embellishment of the city.

The Endicott Building enhanced the appearance of the growing capital and brought the Endicott brothers financial gain. For Gilbert, in addition to nurturing his Minnesota practice, the Endicotts allowed him entree into Boston. With the hostility Gilbert faced after the Minnesota Capitol stone controversies, the East Coast appeared ever more appealing to the ambitious architect.

Alexander S. Porter (1840–1915) and Luther Stearns Cushing (1857–1937) were two key figures in nationwide real-estate development who contributed to the expansion of Gilbert's practice. Porter was instrumental in developing the trust form of ownership.[1] Cushing, a native Bostonian, managed the St. Paul office of the Boston and Northwest Realty Company.[2] Working with Cushing as well as with the Endicott brothers, Gilbert obtained the commission in December of 1896 for the Brazer Building (1896–97) in downtown Boston[3] (fig. 38). Together, Porter and Cushing helped to finance the building, Gilbert's first commission on the East Coast. The well-established construction firm of George A. Fuller Company was the general contractor on the Brazer Building.

38. Cass Gilbert,
Brazer Building,
Boston, Massa-
chusetts, 1896–97.
Photograph by
the author.

Gilbert's eleven-story Brazer Building was surrounded by narrow streets and faced the old Massachusetts State House (1712–13, 1748, 1830). Gilbert provided a restrained facade in this setting. The granite base supports three stories of limestone, with terra-cotta cladding above to match the stone. Oval windows distinguish the top floor and sculpted eagles perch at the cornice level; the building was capped by a gilt bronze *cheneau*.[4]

Many of those involved in the Brazer Building—Gilbert, initially Porter, Cushing, and the Fuller Company—regrouped to collaborate on the Broadway Chambers Building (1899–1900) in New York City (fig. 39). In this structure, the demand for centrally located office space dovetailed with the technical and organizational capacity to supply it. Skyscrapers and monumental government buildings were not just technical achievements: they were also physical manifestations of what Kenneth Boulding called "the organizational revolution."[5] Financial institutions, for example, had established mechanisms that enabled investors to combine and recombine into temporary companies in order to back ambitious building projects.[6] Just as the Brazer Building took two years of planning, so too was the Broadway Chambers Building a scheme on paper for several years before the financial arrangements were firm and Gilbert finally received the commission.

39. Cass Gilbert, Broadway Chambers Building, New York City, 1899–1900. View from southeast c.1905. New-York Historical Society.

Three of the central players in the design and construction of the Broadway Chambers were non–New Yorkers. The Broadway Chambers Building was a real-estate investment for Boston businessman Edward Reynolds Andrews (1831–1916), a man of wide experience and broad interests.[7] Andrews financed the building together with the construction contractor, the George A. Fuller Company, for $500,000. In addition, the Broadway Chambers project launched the New York careers of Harry S. Black, first vice president of the Fuller company,[8] and Cass Gilbert, who was hoping to move his practice from Minnesota to New York. "If this enterprise [the Broadway Chambers] goes through, I will establish my headquarters in New York, and push the work to completion," Gilbert wrote in 1899.[9]

In fact, the Broadway Chambers commission enabled Gilbert to make the long-desired move to New York City. His first design in that city, the structure was a Mediterranean Revival office building in steel, brick, and terra cotta. Its construction in lower Manhattan at the corner of Broadway and Chambers Street characterized rapid commercial building at the turn of the twentieth century. Professionals—the real-estate agent, the contractor, the structural and mechanical engineers, and the architect—contributed their expertise not only to "make a machine to make the land pay" (the final built structure) but also to streamline the construction process.[10]

The Brazer Building provides important information about the design development of the Broadway Chambers Building. Among the Cass Gilbert Papers held in the Minnesota Historical Society is a carbon copy of the Brazer Building specifications that Gilbert edited for the Broadway Chambers project.[11] Of the Brazer design, Gilbert explained in 1897 that "before making my preliminary studies for the exterior design, or even for the plan, I laid out a diagram of the site, and platted what appeared to me the best arrangement of structural work." He noted that he sought a symmetrical subdivision of the facades and that the structural scheme was consistent with symmetry.[12] A similar correspondence between the structural frame and the exterior design exists in the Broadway Chambers project.

An early rendering of the Broadway Chambers done by Gilbert's St. Paul associate Thomas Holyoke in November of 1897 is reminiscent of the Brazer (pl. 8). The drawing shows a building with upper stories clad in a light brick or terra cotta, situated on a double lot. Holyoke's scheme for the New York building also echoed in color and rhythm the arcaded block of the A. T. Stewart Department Store across the street. A year and a half later, in June of 1899, the attempt to acquire more property had failed, so this proposal for a larger site did not materialize.

Another elevation dated 1897 and initialed "CG" was proposed for the corner lot alone, accommodating the client's preferences for dark red brick[13] (pl. 9). While this tripartite scheme and the arcaded base may be traced to earlier buildings, like George B. Post's Havemeyer Building (1891–92) in Manhattan, Gilbert also studied Bruce Price's buildings.[14] Between 1894 and 1896, Price's American Surety Building at Broadway and Pine Street rose twenty-one stories; its all-steel skeleton entirely supported the loads (fig. 40). By 1898, Price's St. James Building at Broadway and Twentieth-sixth Street had been completed. Its colorful shaft featured an arcade at the top.[15] In addition to ideas about color and facade composition adapted from other Manhattan office buildings, Gilbert also drew inspiration for his embellishment of the Broadway and Chambers Street corner from Old World sources. In a retrospective sketch of 1933, Gilbert placed his Broadway Chambers Building next to structures in Utrecht and Venice, stressing their similarities by showing how he had eliminated the top of the Venetian tower and captured the verticality of the Utrecht building (fig. 41).

In February of 1899, after two years of tentative and sporadic meetings involving Alexander Porter, Gilbert, and Andrews, Andrews wrote to Gilbert in Minnesota explaining that the leases on his old building at Broadway and Chambers Street were going to expire the following May.[16] Gilbert lost no time telegraphing Porter and Harry S. Black in New York. He arranged to go to Boston himself in mid-February but asked Porter to deliver his plans beforehand. Just as Gilbert was eager to gain a foothold in New York, so was Harry Black of the Fuller Company. The Broadway Chambers Building was that company's first New York City construction contract.[17] Since Gilbert had worked with Fuller on the Brazer Building, Gilbert wrote Andrews of the company's qualifications: it has "probably built more important office and

40. Bruce Price, American Surety Building, New York City, 1894–96. G. P. Hall and Son, photographers, New-York Historical Society.

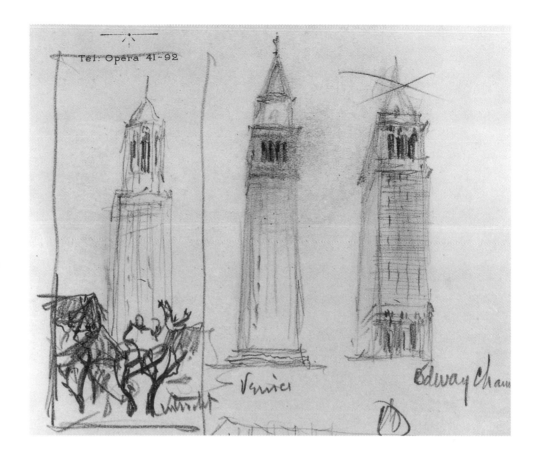

41. Cass Gilbert, pencil sketch of July 13, 1933, comparing Broadway Chambers Building to towers in Utrecht and Venice. Cass Gilbert Collection, Prints and Photographs Collection, Library of Congress.

business buildings than any other firm in the United States."[18] Indeed, Fuller was instrumental in transforming the building industry in America by consolidating construction contracts under its supervision and serving as general contractor.[19] Not only was the Fuller Company a forward-looking construction firm, but it also handled financing and coordinated the building with real-estate interests.[20] In 1899 the Fuller Company put up $100,000 and helped arrange a loan for Andrews.[21]

Edward Andrews had begun working with a New York real-estate agent, Frederick Southack. With Southack and officials from the Fuller Company, primarily Harry Black and Theodore Starrett, Andrews and Gilbert worked out a building scheme that would fully exploit the prominent corner. Black had researched office space needs in lower Manhattan, and he believed that a building such as the Broadway Chambers would net $94,000 annually. Every square foot was a possible source of income, so Black advised Gilbert not to "take up any more space for corridors and halls than is necessary" and to limit the number of elevators to four (which he did).[22]

Southack instigated revisions to Gilbert's scheme. He insisted that the windows of the lower stories be rectangular rather than arched. He specified high ceilings (twelve to sixteen feet) for the bottom three stories, with ten-foot ceilings sufficing for the upper floors. Southack also pressed for increasing the height to twenty stories, but after some discussion, Andrews decided on eighteen. He requested, however, that all of Southack's other suggestions be implemented.[23]

The Broadway Chambers lot measured fifty-one by ninety-four feet. The steel-frame building provided space for three small stores on the ground floor and office spaces above. Typical office floors were subdivided into nine types of spaces, ranging from rooms of about 850 square feet down to those of 170 square feet (fig. 42). While all offices had direct natural lighting, an independent plant for electric lighting was housed in the basement. The arcaded top floors were originally reserved for a club.

The Fuller Company contracted to finish the Broadway Chambers Building in one year, that is, by May 1, 1900. Building rapidly, so that rental losses could be minimized, required the efficient cooperation of many people. Theodore Starrett, who was second vice president of the Fuller Company in 1899 and 1900, supervised the construction of the Broadway Chambers.[24] After the building application was approved and the permit granted on July 12, 1899, construction proceeded with all due haste.[25] The eighteen floors of steel beams were erected quickly once the foundations were in place. To ensure lateral stability (against wind loads of thirty pounds per square foot), deep girders with gusset plates were used in the two narrow walls and on the lower floors of the longer south side.[26]

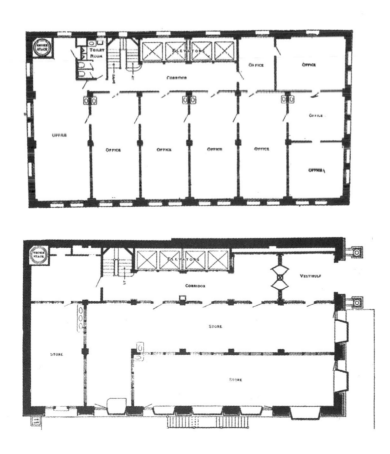

42. Broadway Chambers Building. First-floor plan and typical floor plan. Fireproof Building Construction: Prominent Buildings Erected by the George A. Fuller Company.

The structural engineers on the Broadway Chambers building were Corydon Purdy and Lightner Henderson.[27] Gilbert also collaborated with Reginald Pelham Bolton, the mechanical engineer on the Broadway Chambers project. The building was heated by direct radiation using exhaust steam from two boilers; the plumbing provided for 16 toilet rooms and 102 office basins. The main lines of all risers were concentrated at one point, and were accessible throughout their entire lengths. A fire line had valves and hose reels at every floor as well as on the roof. Bolton's article in the *Engineering Record* of 1899 urged the improvement of mechanical equipment in commercial structures and pressed for the recognition of his specialty: "The importance of the mechanical equipment considerably outweighs the value of any architectural features."[28] Theodore Starrett affirmed this view: "A skyscraper without the boilers is junk above the second floor. In winter it would be uninhabitable."[29]

43. Broadway Chambers Building. View of top-floor bays, Chambers Street side. Photograph by the author.

The three-story base of the Broadway Chambers Building was clad in a rosy Stony Creek granite that had been dressed in long blocks of varying texture. A twelve-story shaft of hard, dark red brick above the base was relieved by the pairs of windows punched in each bay. The top three floors capped the building with a display of polychrome terra cotta.[30] Two-story pilasters with an inset strip of yellow terra cotta rose above the brick shaft to frame the upper-level arches. Windows were recessed behind the arcade, outlined by blue terra-cotta strips. Balconies of gilded wrought iron curved out in front of the sixteenth-story windows, and lampposts with electric globes marked the center of each window (fig. 43). Long red terra-cotta panels punctuated the corners at the outermost bays. Originally, the Broadway Chambers was crowned with a copper *cheneau* with anthemion motifs. The date was left off the facade of the building because, it was explained, in twenty years "it will not show its age and renters will still think it modern."[31]

The urban skyscraper was a commodity, and one of the architect's tasks was to treat that commodity artistically. Gilbert's designs were intended to draw tenants and advertise the locations of renters with memorable architectural imagery. Cass Gilbert's account of the rapid rise of the Broadway Chambers Building reiterated that "one must not lose sight of the fact that the machine [the building] is none the less a useful one because it has a measure of beauty, and that architectural beauty, judged even from the economic standpoint, has an income-bearing value."[32] Gilbert's success on the Broadway Chambers Building was not limited to effective colors, a workable plan, and efficient organization of the design and construction process—though those were not unimportant. The architect was also able to please the client and his real-estate agent and wedge himself into New York architectural circles.

By the time Gilbert moved his family from Minnesota and settled permanently in New York City, he had explored a variety of styles in different types of buildings. While his designs were never carbon copies of previous ones and his ideas were not static, the changes observable in his buildings are changes of

scale or material attributable to function and market considerations rather than to any new design theories. In fact, the remarkable aspect of Gilbert's work over his fifty-year career is its consistency during a time of rapid world change. Gilbert translated traditional materials—stone, brick, terra cotta—into a range of architectural styles by means of carefully executed techniques and thoughtful planning. Low budgets sometimes caused a building to appear spare or even to be left partly unfinished, but plan and massing were consistently viable in his projects. Gilbert's approach was conservative: if it worked, respect it, imitate it, adapt it. One of Gilbert's mentors at M.I.T., William Robert Ware, commented that "people who know of half a dozen ways to do things, all equally admirable and all equally unfamiliar, cannot possibly work as the men did who knew only one way, and knew that perfectly well."[33]

In 1899, after winning the Custom House commission, Gilbert, from New York, wrote to his wife in St. Paul about the upcoming parades and water celebrations for Admiral George Dewey (of Spanish-American War fame), encouraging her to bring the family to join in. "We can have a room at the Holland House and see it all . . . Expense cuts no figure now. We are rich . . . Tell the children my ship really has come in (just ahead of Admiral Dewey's)."[34] Thus with Gilbert's New York commissions, he pulled his practice out of worrisome financial straits. The Gilbert family first lived in an apartment facing Central Park at 48 West Fifty-ninth Street and then, in 1902, moved into a Federal Revival townhouse in another fashionable neighborhood, at 45 East Seventy-eighth Street.[35]

While designing tall with a "measure of beauty" was one challenge for Cass Gilbert, how to plan and embellish civic buildings was another. Tall buildings had met with resistance due to their height and the resulting shadows, crowding, and real-estate competition, not to mention perceived safety and aesthetic problems.[36] The design of civic monuments presented an opposite challenge: how to look grand and imposing without being tall, especially in the context of an increasing number of tall buildings?[37] Gilbert would have the opportunity to contend with this question in his design for the United States Custom House (1899–1907).

Winning the competition in November of 1899 for the U.S. Custom House in New York tested Gilbert's artistic, political, and diplomatic skills. The collector of customs, George Bidwell, was one of the most powerful officials in New York City, presiding as he did over thousands of federal employees who assessed duties at the leading port in America. When Congress decided to build a new home for the huge New York customs operation, the project immediately became ensnarled in politics. Controversy surrounded the site selection, the rules for the design competition, the nomination of the jury, the award to Gilbert, and the letting of construction contracts.[38] Considering the complex layers of municipal and federal government involvement in the design and construction of his Custom House, it is to Gilbert's credit that so fine a building went up[39] (fig. 44).

Even before the Custom House competition was announced in 1899, Gilbert was maneuvering in order to be invited to compete. His former partner, James Knox Taylor, who by then was supervising architect of the United States, was to determine the architects who would be invited to submit designs.[40] Among the twenty competitors, there were four from outside New York; Gilbert made sure he submitted his application from New York to avoid antagonizing New York politicians and architects. Still, there was a flurry of protest when the commission was awarded to the "outsider," Cass Gilbert. To President William McKinley, New York senator Thomas "Boss" Platt tellingly complained that Gilbert "has only recently arrived from Minnesota and is not a member of the Republican organization of the City and County of New York."[41] Gilbert's response was to form clever alliances with officials in Washington and to take advantage of the weakening local machine in New York.

Given the competition Gilbert faced that summer in New York, he decided to submit an elegant Beaux-Arts scheme that was considerably more elaborate than anything he had previously produced. In addition to his experience on the Minnesota State Capitol and his recognized design talents, Gilbert enhanced his chances for triumph in the Custom House competition by hiring staff members who were thoroughly trained in the Beaux-Arts tradition. Samuel-Stevens Haskell was a Minnesotan whom Gilbert had hired in the late 1880s and then had helped to study at the École des Beaux-Arts in Paris. Ernest-Michel Hébrard (1875–1933) was a French Beaux-Arts graduate who was brought to New York by Haskell during the summer of 1899 specifically to assist with the Custom House competition.[42]

Haskell devoted his attention to the plan of the Custom House. The twenty-plus pages of regulations from the United States Treasury Department served as a guide. The government's program called for a central, two-story court, with a U-shaped arrangement of the upper floors. Quickly committing himself to a scheme in which a vaulted rotunda served as the primary volume around which the rest of the building was organized, Haskell then struggled with the architectural problem of containing the modern proliferation of paper.[43] He solved the dilemma of how to store massive quantities of records by treating the inner sections of the eastern and western wings essentially as library stacks.[44] Hébrard, on the other hand, concentrated on the elevations, and, after the commission was gained, Hébrard remained in Gilbert's New York office to work on revisions.

On September 20, 1899, the three-man jury narrowed its choice to two firms, that of Carrère and Hastings and that of Cass Gilbert.[45] Both John Carrère (1858–1911) and Thomas Hastings (1860–1929) had graduated from the Ecole des Beaux-Arts in Paris; and in 1897 they had won the competition for the New York Public Library (built 1902–11). There was one major difference between the plans submitted by Gilbert and those of Carrère and Hastings: Carrère and Hastings had placed the rotunda on the ground floor, while Gilbert had lifted

*44. Cass Gilbert,
United States
Custom House,
New York City,
1899–1907.
Exterior from
Bowling Green
c.1908. G. P. Hall
and Son, photogra-
phers, New-York
Historical Society.*

45. United States Custom House. Longitudinal section. American Architect and Building News.

it to the second floor. What Gilbert did was to raise the "first" floor on a rusticated base, so that visitors ascended to the main floor from the exterior (fig. 45). Gilbert noted that the jury valued this choice.[46] After a flurry of debate, Gilbert finally was awarded the commission on November 4, 1899.

Gilbert's design was revised numerous times over the next two years. Just after he submitted his scheme to the jury on September 18, 1899, he reassessed the plan and elevation graphically on September 22 (figs. 46 and 47). He often would sketch an elevation or a plan, send the drawings to his New York office, and have them "take it up in this spirit."[47] A crisp elevation done by William P. Foulds and dated January 23, 1900, reduced the number of columns and simplified the roof (pl. 10). An undated, elegantly facile rendering of the Bowling Green facade signed by Thomas R. Johnson, who became increasingly important as a member of Gilbert's design team, was probably done shortly after a mansard roof was restored[48] (pl. 11).

Foulds (1879–?) and Johnson (1872–1915) would play important roles in Gilbert's office for the next fifteen years. Foulds had been hired as a young student in 1899, and his drawing style became surer and more relaxed as he gained experience.[49] Johnson came to Gilbert in 1900 already a skilled draftsman. His sketches capture textures and dimensions of various buildings to clarify the colors, shadows, and profiles of the designs. Johnson, like Gilbert, could draw quickly and well, shaping an idea in a sketch that could be worked up by another, less experienced staff member. Johnson's role in Gilbert's office was significant, and his early death in 1915 was a major blow.[50]

Gilbert stressed the prominence of the Custom House in New York City by taking full advantage of its site on the small Bowling Green park with Broadway extending north. The building's proximity to the waterfront and adjacent open space allowed for light, air, and views. Conceiving of the structure as a decorated ensemble with a full sculptural program, varied and excellent materials, and fine craftsmanship, Gilbert surrounded visitors to the granite Custom House with marble sculptures and colorful mosaics as they climbed the broad stairs to the entrance. Visitors then entered a majestic vaulted interior, rich with ornament and expensive materials that actively engaged their senses as they conducted their transactions. Thus daily customs business turned away from the nearby workaday harbor and instead was conducted in a building purposefully oriented toward the city.[51] Gilbert turned the prosaic into grandeur in his Custom House design.

The monumental seven-story structure, produced at a cost of $5,130,000, gave expression to American commercial power when it opened in 1907.[52] Imported marble columns and marble mosaic floors lent elegance to the main lobby on the second level. The entry also featured crisply carved marble fountains just under lively iron grilles that covered the windows facing into the court. The three central bays of the transverse lobby rose two stories into groin vaults painted with nautical motifs. Thin timbrel tile arches constructed according to a method perfected by Rafael Guastavino supported the main stairs that wound up through the seven stories of the interior.[53] Elaborate plaster panels covered the tilework. Paintings, carved wood panels, chandeliers, and a custom-designed fireplace distinguished the first-floor reception room and offices of the collector of customs. Other offices angled down the sides of the building; the rear wing, only three stories in height, was occupied by a branch post office.

46 (below left). United States Custom House. Sketches of exterior elevation and decoration, September 22, 1899. Cass Gilbert Collection, Manuscripts Division, Library of Congress.

47 (below right). United States Custom House. Sketch of first-floor plan, September 22, 1899. Cass Gilbert Collection, Manuscripts Division, Library of Congress.

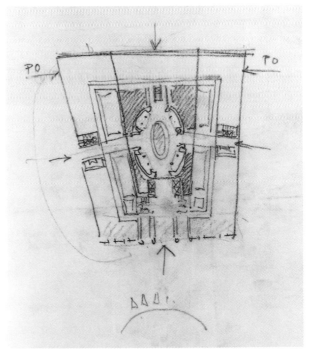

*48. United States
Custom House.
Rotunda interior.
Museum of the
City of New York.*

Elegant materials and lavish decoration in the Custom House emphasized the prosperity of the ports of New York and New Jersey. The elliptical rotunda was the focus of the Custom House plan and the hub of its public activity. As in many modern traditionalist buildings, grand appearances were supported by modern steel construction and other refined techniques. Special steel tension ring girders were milled to accommodate the vaulted ceilings that penetrated the dome of the elliptical rotunda at four points. These horizontal rings helped support a one-hundred-ton skylight that sliced through the dome. This remarkable dome (135 by 85 feet) rose over the two-story rotunda utilizing Rafael Guastavino's method of thin-vault construction (fig. 48). In this case, a double shell of flat tiles laid in Portland cement curved up to meet the framing for the skylight.[54]

The John Peirce Company received the contract for the Custom House superstructure and promised to execute the work in two and one-half years. Some bids lower than Peirce's proposed using limestone instead of granite. Gilbert favored a granite building, as did collector George Bidwell. "A strong public sentiment exists in New York that the building should be of granite . . . The granite which most nearly fills the requirements in color, quality, and price is the Fox Island granite, offered by John Peirce."[55] Thick, self-supporting exterior walls of granite backed with brick carried adjacent floor and roof loads.[56] A steel framework supported the remaining hollow tile floors and roofs. On the seventh story, box girders supported trusses for the mansard roof.

The Custom House construction contract introduced Gilbert to Peirce, with whom he would work over the next seven years not only on the Custom House but also on the West Street Building (1905–7) in New York. Both men maintained a calm professional demeanor as they transformed the stone into a "fruitcake of Maine granite," as Ada Louise Huxtable, writing almost seventy years later, described the New York Custom House.[57] Gilbert was often alarmed at the slow delivery of stone, a main reason for the building's completion two years behind schedule. Gilbert even sent his staff to Maine to examine the quarries' methods and determine how the work might be hastened (fig. 49). On one visit, George Wells, Gilbert's superintendent of construction, criticized the quarries for cutting stone in a sequence convenient to them but not appropriate to the needs of the building as it progressed.[58]

To ensure good proportions and strong details on the Custom House, Gilbert initiated a "new departure in [the] construction of public buildings" by having Peirce erect a full-size plaster model of a section of the facade on the site.[59] After he inspected the full-scale model, Gilbert simplified some of the consoles, frieze ornament, and other carving.[60] Plaster models for the capitals were shipped to the quarry itself.[61]

Consciously reviving the Renaissance principle of collaboration, Gilbert assigned the decoration of the Custom House to over one dozen artists. He convinced the government of the merits of planning all the work in advance so that a minimum of changes would be required. "A precedent for this line of action is found in the Library of Congress," he wrote in 1901.[62] Among the artists who worked on the Custom House, the best known is

49. Granite cutting shed at Vinalhaven, Maine, quarry, c.1904, as work proceeds on Gilbert's United States Custom House in New York City. New-York Historical Society.

50. Cass Gilbert with John DuFais, Union Club (demolished), New York City, 1901–3. New-York Historical Society.

Daniel Chester French, who was responsible for "The Four Continents" in front of the building.[63]

Gilbert won another competition in 1900, when the Custom House revisions were well underway, the Minnesota State Capitol was midway through construction, and the Broadway Chambers Building was almost finished: the prestigious Union Club (1901–3) at Fifty-first Street and Fifth Avenue in Manhattan (fig. 50). This project was unusual because of Gilbert's association with John DuFais, an architect with good social connections and therefore valuable; Gilbert usually avoided such partnerships.[64] Thomas Johnson, still new to Gilbert's office, revised the Union Club competition elevations. His sketch of the Fifty-first Street facade is similar to the carefully proportioned *palazzo* that was completed in 1903[65] (fig. 51).

Samuel-Stevens Haskell gloated to Gilbert:

> It does seem as if it were almost impossible to lose in competitions—two out of 3 in one year [they had lost the Washington University competition] is an excellent record, especially when one considers the prominence of the two buildings, their location, and the interest that the public take [*sic*] in them.[66]

Given the successes of Gilbert's firm, the architect had to expand his office beyond rehiring Haskell and "floaters" like Hébrard. Gilbert hired two government employees, Gunvald Aus and George Wells. Aus (1861?–1950) had been a structural engineer in the Office of the Supervising Architect since

1895. Wells (dates unknown) came to Gilbert's office from the New York City Office of Repairs. Both men became long-time associates of Gilbert's. Delegating structural engineering to Aus, Custom House supervision to Wells, and office management to Haskell freed Gilbert to oversee his projects across the nation and to seek further commissions.[67]

On a smaller scale than the New York Custom House, but with the same spirit of artistic cooperation and civic advancement, Gilbert's Essex County Courthouse in Newark, New Jersey, was completed in 1902 (figs. 52 and 53). Andrew O'Connor was commissioned to do the sculptural ornament, and interior murals were executed by Edwin Blashfield, Kenyon Cox, Howard Pyle, and Frank Millet (fig. 55).[68] Gilbert had entered the closed competition for the courthouse in Newark in November of 1901, and was awarded the commission that December.[69] The plan organized offices on the exterior and courtrooms around a domed rotunda. The exterior of the courthouse was South Dover white marble, with granite approaches. The slope leading up to the courthouse had the effect of diminishing the building somewhat, so Gilbert altered the image of the courthouse through the use of curved stairs. The exterior column entasis was carefully handled as well.

Once Gilbert secured a job in a city, others often followed. In Newark, he designed and executed at least four other buildings in the first two decades of the twentieth century. One was the American Insurance Company Building

51. Union Club. Fifty-first Street elevation sketch on trace by Thomas R. Johnson. New-York Historical Society.

70

52. Cass Gilbert, Essex County Courthouse, Newark, New Jersey, 1901–2. Main facade. Newark Public Library Photograph.

53. Essex County Courthouse. View showing approach. Newark Public Library Photograph.

(1902–5), begun just as the Essex County Courthouse was nearing completion; it looked exceptionally secure (fig. 54). Windows were tightly framed by engaged columns, and an attic story above a prominent cornice emphasized the horizontality of the three-story building.[70] Designing in limestone for this fire insurance company, with the massing and the proportions more important than ornament, gave Gilbert useful insights that he would soon put to use in St. Louis.

Gilbert's Broadway Chambers Building, United States Custom House, Union Club, Essex County Courthouse, and American Insurance Company Building were built on different sites, in two different cities, yet each helped to enliven the urban space around them through sophisticated proportions, elegant decoration, and varying colors and textures. These buildings were modern in their locations and functions, yet traditional in their stylistic treatments. French Beaux-Arts design methods, which Gilbert had encountered at M.I.T. with Létang, in the office of McKim, Mead and White, and among his own employees, stressed the composition of the whole building, in plan, elevation, and section. Gilbert's skillful adaptation of the French approach integrated his individual projects with their sites and, in turn, to the greatest extent possible, connected those sites to the larger urban environment. While there are many ways to embellish the city, Cass Gilbert modeled his designs on European precedents that were familiar, pleasing, and reassuring to the client and, often, to members of the public as well.

54. Cass Gilbert, American Insurance Company Building, Newark, New Jersey, 1902–5 (demolished 1981). Newark Public Library Photograph.

*55. Essex County
Courthouse.
Stair hall showing
pendentive paint-
ings by Kenyon
Cox. Newark
Public Library
Photograph.*

CHAPTER 3

LEADERSHIP IN CIVIC DESIGN
Nationwide Commissions

Cass Gilbert's national leadership in civic design was distinguished not only by attempting to satisfy the demands of a particular project but by addressing broader contextual issues as well. To execute a high-quality architectural design is extraordinarily difficult, considering the enormous number of competing and, often, conflicting interests involved. Heading the list is the large financial investment required, which is affected by the needs and wishes of all the parties: clients, users, investors, suppliers, contractors, engineers, and regulators, to name some participants. The architect, then, faces the daunting task of producing a design that will satisfy most of the competing concerns. But expectations really go beyond the satisfactory completion of one building. That building is also expected to enhance the ever-changing built environment and is often evaluated in terms of its contributions to traffic flow, respectful scale, visual delight, and urban spatial definition.

Until 1901, Gilbert had had little experience with the planning of large schemes. He had been involved minimally in the 1893 World's Columbian Exposition in Chicago as an architecture juror, but it was not until the Louisiana Purchase Exposition (1904) in St. Louis that he was able to tackle planning for an ensemble of buildings.[1] The last half of the nineteenth century was an era of large expositions, in Europe especially, that featured the accomplishments of individual nations in huge, expansive buildings arranged in parklike settings. Among the most famous of these are the Great Exhibition of 1851, held in London, and the Paris Exhibition of 1889, as well as the World's Columbian Exposition. In addition to providing showcases for industrial, agricultural, and cultural achievements, these fairs often were remarkable for their architecture and engineering.

Plans for the exposition were underway in 1901. The Louisiana Purchase Exposition Company was organized by May of that year, with nine major

56. Cass Gilbert, Palace of Fine Arts (Art Building), Louisiana Purchase Exposition, St. Louis, Missouri, 1901–4. Detail of initial study with dome, October 5, 1901. New-York Historical Society.

RT BUILDING ST. LOUIS EXPOSIT

SCALE 1/16 INCH PER FOOT.

committees set up to coordinate the exposition around the theme of "The Progress of Man since the Louisiana Purchase." William H. Thompson was chairman of the committee on grounds and buildings, and he, in turn, assembled a commission of architects, with St. Louis architect Isaac S. Taylor as director of works. Gilbert was a member of the thirteen-person commission.[2] Emmanuel Masqueray was appointed in September 1901 to coordinate construction at the site, which encompassed 1,240 hilly acres (twice the size of the 1893 Chicago exposition), about six miles from the Mississippi River in Forest Park, now at the western edge of the city.[3] Gilbert chaired the committee that created the site plan; other members of this committee included Frank Howe, C. Howard Walker, and John Carrère.[4] Gilbert was familiar with part of the site because he had entered the 1899 competition for the campus of Washington University, the property of which adjoined the exposition's site. (That competition was won by the Philadelphia firm of Cope and Stewardson.)

Eight of the twelve large exposition buildings fanned out on the hillside (fig. 57). A visitor could take in the whole picture, from the exhibit halls arrayed between landscaped gardens, curved walkways, cascading water, and fountains, to Gilbert's domed Festival Hall (1904) on the hill. Because the lines of the three main streets leading up the hill met at a point three hundred feet behind the convergence of the building axes, the perspective was distorted by terraces curving out from Gilbert's lavish building. This solution was similar to his use of curved stairs at the Essex County Courthouse site, only on a larger scale.[5]

In addition to working on the site plan, Gilbert received commissions to design two of the exposition buildings in St. Louis: the Palace of Fine Arts (1901–4; known as the Art Building, this structure afterward became the St. Louis Art Museum) and Festival Hall, a temporary pavilion for drama and music.[6] Desire for a dome as well as wings that established minor axes had determined the organization of the original sketches for the Art Building, but those were rejected as being too expensive. Still, the scheme for Festival Hall evolved out of those early designs[7] (figs. 56, 58, and 59). Festival Hall, dismantled in 1905, was an exuberant hall capping the hill of the exposition grounds, inspired in part by the neo-Baroque designs of the 1900 Universal Exposition in Paris[8] (fig. 60). The picturesque setting, with the building reflected in the calm basin of water below, contributed to Festival Hall's success[9] (pl. 12). A crested and pinched dome, 145 feet in diameter at its widest point, rested on a drum pierced with oculus windows. The highlights and shadows of ornamental urns, masks, and putti and the deeply set windows gave solidity to Festival Hall, which housed an auditorium of four thousand seats, a large stage with accompanying dressing rooms and service facilities, and an organ chamber.

The Art Building, just behind Festival Hall, was far more closed in upon itself and restrained in its ornament.[10] In contrast to the ivory white staff of Festival

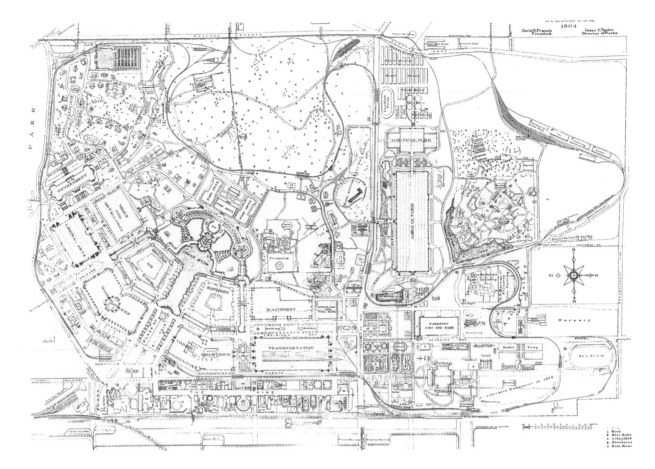

57. Cass Gilbert, with John Carrère, Frank Howe, and C. Howard Walker, plan of the Louisiana Purchase Exposition, St. Louis, Missouri, 1904. St. Louis Art Museum.

58. Palace of Fine Arts, Louisiana Purchase Exposition. Initial study with dome, October 5, 1901. New-York Historical Society.

59. Palace of Fine Arts, Louisiana Purchase Exposition. "One of first sketches for art building," October 5, 1901. New-York Historical Society.

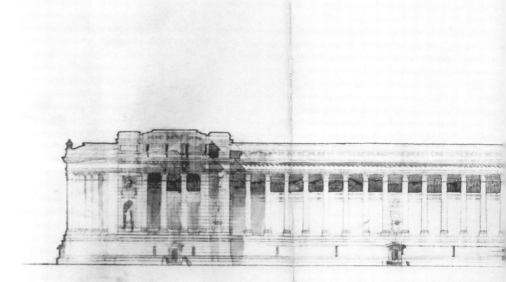

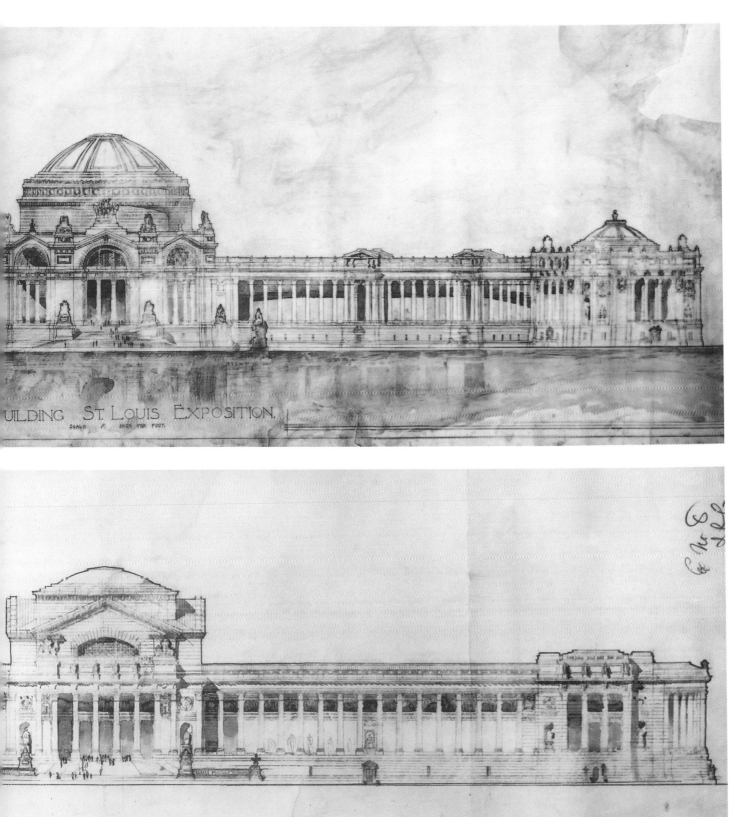

UILDING ST. LOUIS EXPOSITION.
SCALE ⅛ INCH PER FOOT.

DING ST. LOUIS EXPOSITION
SCALE ⅛" PER FOOT.

Festival Hall.

Hall, the central portion of the Art Building was built of limestone and brick to house permanently the collections of the St. Louis Art Museum.[11] Two temporary brick buildings flanked the central section, forming an 850-foot facade (fig. 61). This north front was unrelieved by fenestration, except for the thermal windows that opened up the gables of the central pavilion[12] (fig. 62).

That Gilbert's commissions for the Louisiana Purchase Exposition were related to French exhibition structures and Grand Prix projects is not a coincidence. No doubt Gilbert's office studied Charles Atwood's Fine Arts Building for the 1893 World's Columbian Exposition, a structure that was derived quite directly from Emile Bénard's 1867 winning entry to the Grand Prix competition, "A Palace for an Exhibition of Fine Arts."[13] Gilbert's employee John Rachac had returned from the Ecole des Beaux-Arts in 1902, and Thomas Johnson was abroad briefly in 1903. Johnson's sketches for Festival Hall reveal his central role in the project, and Rachac attended many meetings in St. Louis on Gilbert's behalf.[14] The director of the St. Louis Art Museum, Halsey Cooley Ives, was not impressed, however, with all the Beaux-Arts trappings. Ives had served as art director for the World's Columbian Exposition and reflected that "every dollar used in Chicago was expended in structure itself, while in the case of the problem assigned to Mr. Gilbert, the

60 (opposite). Cass Gilbert, Festival Hall (dismantled) for Louisiana Purchase Exposition, St Louis, Missouri, 1904. Exterior. Missouri Historical Society.

61. Palace of Fine Arts, Louisiana Purchase Exposition. Exterior view showing temporary pavilions. Missouri Historical Society.

62. Palace of Fine Arts, Louisiana Purchase Exposition. North entrance pavilion. Photograph by the author.

building proper is connected with a decorative scheme which has no value whatever as an exhibition structure."[15]

The plan for the permanent Art Building was insistently symmetrical. The main sculpture gallery bisected a long rectangle containing the galleries. Sculpture Hall, the centerpiece of the main building, was lit by six arched clerestory windows and round skylights in the niches below the windows (fig. 63). Casts of monumental sculpture were lined up under the seventy-eight-foot-high barrel-vaulted ceiling. The vault was of Guastavino tile construction; the texture of the tile, the thermal windows, and the top-lit niches gave the space the character of ancient Roman baths.[16] The hall is only eighty feet long, however, so the scale of the space is far from imperial. Still, Gilbert evoked in his museum the monumental space of the Baths of Caracalla, which he had rendered in a watercolor study in 1880 (pl. 13).

No clear path directed the visitor through the galleries. Instead, a sequence of options was presented, including doorways leading to the temporary pavilions that extended to the south around a garden court. The court, defined by the brick walls of the temporary pavilions and the south front of the permanent building, featured plaster casts in an informal display. Broad eaves extended out from the walls to shade visitors from the summer sun; Spanish architectural details recalled Mediterranean prototypes.

Festival Hall provided an impressive introduction to the processional space of the Art Building's Sculpture Hall. The structures themselves were built so closely together that they seemed to form a single composition. Indeed, this closeness posed its own problem: Gilbert argued that he had designed two buildings and only been paid for one. This was one of his few commissions to end in a lawsuit.[17] On March 30, 1905, Gilbert wrote to his wife:

> Judge Lehman, one of the Directors of the Exposition Company, was in court this afternoon and when I came off the stand he came up to be introduced to me and expressed his entire sympathy with my contention . . . and ended by saying he is chairman of the Public Library Board of St. Louis and invites me to be one of the competitors in a limited and paid competition . . . here (which invitation I have accepted provisionally.)[18]

This library job would not materialize for another two years, but Lehman's sympathetic response is an example of how Gilbert's practice grew, even through litigation.

At the 1904 exposition in St. Louis, Gilbert joined other prominent architects to create a spectacular tableau in Forest Park. Of that temporary ensemble, only his limestone Art Building remains, on the crest of the hill that served to organize the exposition plan. Due to the restricted budget, the building's spatial volumes and proportions carry more interest than its decorative detail. Now the St. Louis Art Museum, it has been expanded and reinterpreted in what might be called the "perpetual discovery" of the architectural process.[19]

63. Palace of Fine Arts, Louisiana Purchase Exposition. Sculpture Hall. Missouri Historical Society.

64. Cass Gilbert, facade and plan studies for the Cathedral of St. Paul, January 22, 1905, in letter to Julia Gilbert. Gilbert noted that the inspirations were Romanesque, listing Clermont-Ferrand for the apse, Coutances for the towers, and Arles for the porch. Cass Gilbert Collection, Manuscripts Division, Library of Congress.

Gilbert continued to compose buildings into ensembles after the Louisiana Purchase Exposition. Sometimes, as at Oberlin College in Ohio, the building commissions were spaced over twenty-five years; in other cases, in New Haven, Connecticut, Austin, Texas, and Detroit, Michigan, for example, Gilbert's buildings were intended to be part of a larger plan that was never carried out. In two instances, the Minneapolis campus of the University of Minnesota (1908) and a scheme for the area around City Hall Park (1923) in Manhattan, Gilbert's plans resulted in no buildings by him whatsoever.[20] By 1905, when he received the first commission from Oberlin College, his experience with earlier competitions for campus plans, as well as with the exposition in St. Louis, had prepared him for the design of multiple, related buildings.

Finney Chapel (1905–8) was the first of five buildings Cass Gilbert designed for Oberlin College[21] (pl. 14). Its final form suffered from a radically reduced budget, so that a tall tower was diminished and the interior was never completed. As Gilbert was preparing the designs for Finney Chapel, he was also thinking about the design for Minnesota's Roman Catholic cathedral in St. Paul. While he decided not to enter the fray for the cathedral, to be built on a hill overlooking the Minnesota Capitol, Gilbert did sketch a facade in a letter to his wife[22] (fig. 64). Ideas from this scheme and its precedents—medieval churches in southern France—echo quietly in the Finney Memorial Chapel[23] (fig. 65).

Of the final version, Gilbert wrote that "The facade is very simple . . . not unlike some of the early Italian churches."[24] The stone carver was instructed to emulate Northern Italian Romanesque but also was given photographs of Byzantine capitals and asked to imitate the vigorous, deeply cut foliage.[25] Gilbert recalled traveling in Italy: "I stayed a little while at Assisi and was much impressed with the architecture . . . there and in Perugia [which] requires exceedingly simple lines and very broad, plain surfaces. It admits of very rich decoration at focal points and of rich color decoration."[26] While the Finney chapel's exterior was simple, with decoration concentrated on the arcaded entry, Gilbert intended that the interior be richly colored, although the scheme was not executed for lack of funds (pl. 15). Arthur B. Willett of Willett and Schultz prepared a sketch for the interior that had a warmth and texture in contrast to the spare exterior. Gilbert accommodated Oberlin's wish to provide a large gathering space for both religious and secular services by making the chapel sanctuary like an auditorium. This large unencumbered volume calls to mind the interior of the Dayton Avenue Presbyterian Church, of two decades before.

The next decade brought Gilbert the opportunity to design the Allen Memorial Art Building on Oberlin's campus and to elaborate on the red and off-white Amherst sandstone decoration used for Finney Chapel's exterior[27] (1914–17; fig. 66). Appointed campus architect for Oberlin College in 1911,

65. Cass Gilbert, Finney Memorial Chapel, Oberlin College, Oberlin, Ohio, 1905–8. Main portal. Photograph by the author.

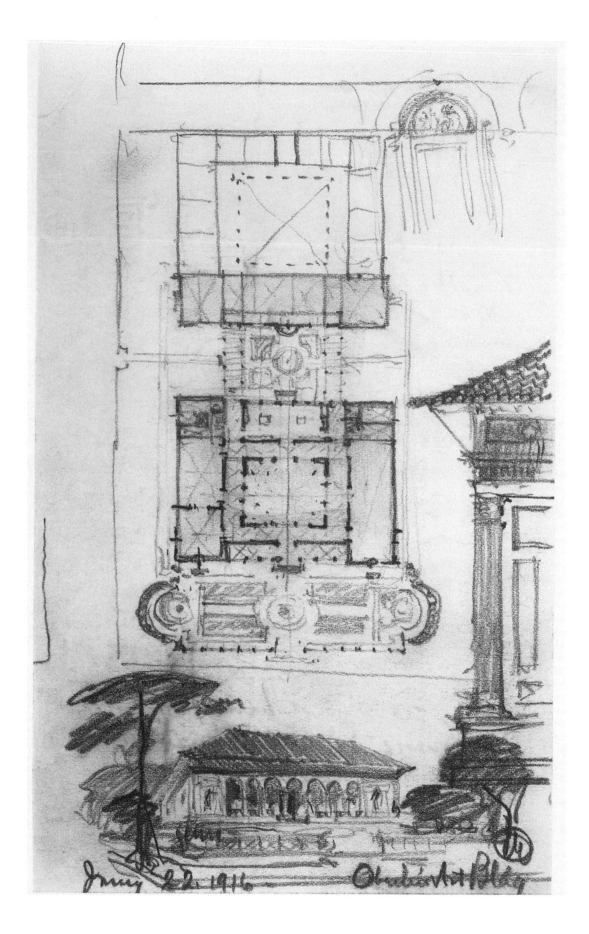

Gilbert designed the Cox Administration Building (1914–15) at the same time as the Allen Memorial Art Building.[28] For all of his buildings at Oberlin, Gilbert drew on Romanesque, Gothic, and early Renaissance works from southern France and northern Italy. Gilbert generally preferred Mediterranean classicism for educational institutions and libraries as a means of celebrating Western humanistic learning as he understood it.

For the Allen Memorial Art Building, Gilbert adapted Filippo Brunelleschi's Foundling Hospital (1419–45) in Florence by quoting its familiar, delicately proportioned arcaded loggia (fig. 67). Tuscan light seemed to inspire his pastel sketch of the design; the brilliant colors evoke a sunlit Mediterranean landscape (pl. 16). Inscribed on the wall over one niche are the words: "The Fine Arts, A Heritage from the Past."

Passing beneath the mosaic-lined vaults of the loggia, visitors entered a two-story sculpture hall lit by clerestory windows and flanked by top-lit galleries to each side (fig. 68). Gilbert also provided a contemplative place beyond the galleries, a small courtyard with a fountain (fig. 69). Reminiscent of a cloister he had sketched in Monreale, Italy, in 1902, the Allen Memorial Art Building courtyard is an intimate, calm space for reflection (pl. 17). Classrooms, a library, and art studios completed the museum program, so that after an initiation to historical works, visitors could apply the lessons in their own manner.[29]

Gilbert used color to good effect in his Oberlin museum. A polychrome terra-cotta frieze and relief sculpture distinguish the loggia entrance; the unfenestrated, buff sandstone walls are subdivided by niches with marble vases and enlivened by squares and rectangles outlined in red sandstone. This sensitivity to color, as well as the general massing of the Allen Memorial Art Building, links it to Gilbert's near-contemporary designs for the University of Texas at Austin.

Oberlin's art building provided classrooms and studios in addition to library and museum space. As that project was nearing completion, Gilbert received a commission from a corporation of painters in New York City to provide studio and living space for them. The Rodin Studio Apartment building (1916–17) at 200 West Fifty-seventh Street in New York City contrasts with the low, subtle Allen Memorial Art Building[30] (fig. 70). This reinforced-concrete frame building was covered in brick and distinguished by terra-cotta and cast-iron ornament. The corbel table cornices were also terra cotta. The way in which the central studio apartments were interlocked, with a two-story studio fitting over a single-story bedroom or bathroom, produced an alternating pattern of elaborate spandrels on the Fifty-seventh Street front that animated the surface of a rather plain box. Furthermore, Gilbert used pronounced terra-cotta mullions with vertical pieces set in front of them that were attached to the spandrels and capped by winged figures. Gothic-inspired canopies of cast and wrought iron projected out from the facade, catching light and creating shadows. The first-floor entrance, which led to shops, second-floor offices,

66. Cass Gilbert, Allen Memorial Art Building, Oberlin College, Oberlin, Ohio, 1914–17. Sheet showing plan, perspective with landscaping, and exterior detail, January 22, 1916. Cass Gilbert Collection, Prints and Photographs Division, Library of Congress.

68. Allen Memorial Art Building. Main hall. Courtesy of the Oberlin College Archives, Oberlin College.

69. Allen Memorial Art Building. Courtyard. Courtesy of the Oberlin College Archives, Oberlin College.

and the apartments, was highlighted by polychrome terra cotta.[31] The studios were oriented to provide maximum light for the artists.

Outside of New York, and in addition to his work at Oberlin College, Gilbert had other opportunities to plan architectural groupings. In 1907 he was hired along with Frederick Law Olmsted Jr. to prepare a city plan for the New Haven, Connecticut, Civic Improvement Committee, headed by George Dudley Seymour.[32] Presented in 1909–10, the scheme was almost completely ignored, but Gilbert at least received the commission for the public library (1908–11) on New Haven's Green and for the New York, New Haven and Hartford Railroad Station (1909–18).

Gilbert set the brick and marble Ives Memorial Library back from the street and raised the entry level up on a podium accessible by way of grand stairs, amplifying the scale of New Haven's Georgian architecture (fig. 71). The interior is distinguished by an oval vestibule flanked by curving staircases. While a public library, the scale of the interior spaces has the grace and delicacy of eighteenth-century residential architecture.[33]

The completion of the New Haven station (now called Union Station) for the New York, New Haven and Hartford Railroad line was considerably delayed (fig. 72). The initial planning for this station was begun about the same time as Gilbert was designing the Ives Memorial Library and consulting

70 (opposite). Cass Gilbert, Rodin Studio Apartment building (200 West Fifty-seventh Street), New York City, 1916–17 Construction photograph. Cass Gilbert Collection, Archives Center, National Museum of American History, Smithsonian Institution.

71. Cass Gilbert, Ives Memorial Library, New Haven, Connecticut, 1908–11. American Architect and Building News.

with Frederick Law Olmsted Jr. and the Civic Improvement Committee about a comprehensive plan for New Haven (1907–10). As Gilbert's associate John R. Rockart (formerly known as John R. Rachac Jr.) explained in a presentation to the American Institute of Architects in 1909, the location of the station was determined by "conditions such as length of trains, the curves and grades, a slight elevation at the station platform to facilitate starting and stopping of trains and providing accommodations for the branch roads with long straight sidings on the city side."[34] Gilbert and his associates had hoped that a semicircular space in front of the station could be connected to the Green at the center of the city by a new avenue. The scheme fell through and the station remains a rather spare brick block distinguished by a slightly projecting central pavilion with five arches, flanked by five narrow, fenestrated bays on each side, and an attic story above a limestone cornice.[35]

While Rockart noted that a train station was "the vestibule of the city," in New Haven's case there was a lengthy corridor that preceded this vestibule.[36] The New York, New Haven and Hartford Railroad line, carrying both passengers and freight, began along the Harlem River in the Bronx. Cass Gilbert's firm designed twelve suburban train depots for the company in 1907–8, all quite picturesque and different, but only half of that number was built.[37] Two sketches, of the Port Morris and Pelham Manor depots, both dated 1907, show the variety of Gilbert's designs. Each station met different local requirements. For example, at Port Morris, the depot was built against an elevated road (fig. 73). Passengers could enter at the street level and ascend to the train tracks on the upper level. This five-bay, two-story depot is more formal and imposing than the others. Pelham Manor, by contrast, has a rough-hewn, squat tower at the entrance and stretches out along the tracks (fig. 74). Its low, tiled roof parallels the tracks, sheltering waiting rooms, service areas, and porches. The Hunts Point depot was built upon a street bridge that had been widened sufficiently to serve the needs of the passengers. At Westchester Avenue, part of the depot is on the ground, while the rest is elevated above the tracks.

As more commissions came to Gilbert without his having to push as hard for them, he devoted more of his time to personal interests and to his country home. In 1907 the Gilberts had purchased a Colonial-era building in Ridgefield, Connecticut, known as the Keeler Tavern. The two-story frame structure had been built in 1766 and was purchased in 1769 by Timothy Keeler. Gilbert added a garden pavilion and a large ell.[38] His interest in his own family genealogy led him back to his roots in New England and Scotland and also prompted him to join ancestral and patriotic clubs like the Society of the Cincinnati.[39] While not unusual for the time, Gilbert's Anglo-Saxonism had a racist component. For example, in 1929 Gilbert wrote to his son: "I want now to build up the office morale and reconstruct the office organization in the drafting room especially—I want to get gentlemen in the organization—not 'kikes,' floaters, or German jews."[40] These repugnant beliefs undoubtedly affected Gilbert's hiring practices. Power with prejudice, then and now, horrifically narrows human lives. Still, it is not a reason to reject the built results of Gilbert's practice; there are many ways to reclaim it.[41]

During the first decade of the twentieth century, Gilbert reached the top of his profession. Not only did he cross the country on trains, visiting clients and job sites in Missouri, Ohio, Michigan, and Texas, in addition to executing the commissions he received on the East Coast, he continued his commitment to professional organizations. He rejoined the Architectural League of New York in 1905 and served as its president from 1913 to 1914.[42] He was elected first to the Institute (1906) then the Academy (1914) of Arts and Letters, serving as president of the American Academy and Institute of Arts and Letters from 1918 to 1920. From 1908 to 1909, Gilbert was president of the American Institute of Architects. In 1908 he was elected to the National Academy of Design; he would become the first architect to be its president (1926–32). As a "joiner" with a mission to help shape the organizations in which he was a member, Gilbert reflected: "Each honor that one receives is a new mortgage upon one's energies—a new obligation to society."[43] In the year that Gilbert acquired his Connecticut home, the New York Custom House and the twenty-three-story West Street Building (discussed below) were completed, and he received commissions for the public library in New Haven, Connecticut, as well as another in St. Louis, Missouri.

Early twentieth-century designers had had numerous opportunities to explore library solutions as many cities built anew or upgraded their municipal libraries.[44] Two well-publicized examples included the Boston Public Library by McKim, Mead and White (1888–95; fig. 75) and the New York Public Library

73 (overleaf). Cass Gilbert, Port Morris Depot of the New York, New Haven and Hartford Railroad, the Bronx, New York, 1907–8. Sketches of four exteriors. Cass Gilbert Collection, Prints and Photographs Division, Library of Congress.

Studies for Port Morri
Station - N.Y. N.H. & H.
the Bronx New York

A Vaillane ♥ Riens Impossible

74. Cass Gilbert, Pelham Manor Depot of the New York, New Haven and Hartford Railroad, Pelham Manor, New York, 1907–8. Sketch of front facade and perspective, June 27, 1907. Cass Gilbert Collection, Prints and Photographs Division, Library of Congress.

75. McKim, Mead and White, Boston Public Library, Boston, Massachusetts, 1888–95. New-York Historical Society.

76. Cass Gilbert, St. Louis Public Library, St. Louis, Missouri, 1907–12. Construction photograph looking northeast. St. Louis Public Library Archives.

(1902–11) by Carrère and Hastings.[45] Gilbert's St. Louis Public Library, which opened in January 1912, differed significantly from the McKim, Mead and White Boston prototype. While the new St. Louis library gave a nod to the exterior elevation of the Boston library, a scheme derived from Italian Renaissance *palazzi* and Henri Labrouste's Bibliothèque Ste.-Geneviève in Paris, Gilbert deviated sharply from his mentors' plan (fig. 76).

Andrew Carnegie gave $500,000 in 1901 for St. Louis to build a new library and six branches. The 1907 limited competition for the design of the central library included nine firms; the jury was composed of three architects.[46] After the designs were narrowed to five finalists, the firms were asked to revise their initial schemes. In his winning scheme, Cass Gilbert, for example, changed a semicircular delivery hall to a large oblong, recognizing that, while it would cost more initially, it would avoid a difficult addition later.[47] His emphasis on the delivery area won praise and challenged the prominence given to the reading room in Boston's library.

The central branch of the St. Louis Public Library (1907–12) is near downtown, on the southern half of what was known as Missouri Park. Set back seventy feet from Olive Street, the approaches past balustrades and across granite terraces were thoughtfully composed. Broad granite steps, light standards, sculpture, and now plantings pace the visitor's progress (pl. 19).

77. St. Louis Public Library. First- and main-floor plans. American Architect and Building News.

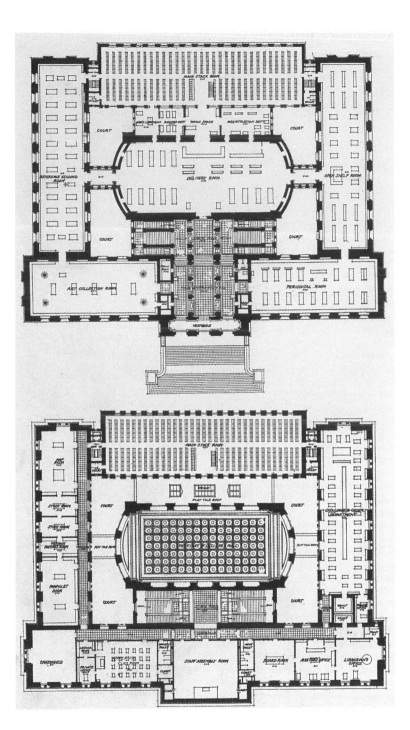

The plan is essentially a square with inner courtyards formed by a two-story delivery hall placed within the square (fig. 77). The main entrance is marked by a projecting pavilion with three arches leading to an entry vestibule.[48] Six arcaded windows on either side of the entry continue the rhythm and provide light to the art collection and periodical room. Below and above the two-story arched windows on three sides are square windows that illuminate the ground and third stories. The decoration of the granite facade pays homage to printers and classic literature.[49]

Visitors enter the library from Olive Street. Straight ahead from the vaulted, marble entry are the stair hall and delivery hall beyond; to the left, the art collection; to the right, the periodical room. Clusters of electric lights behind alabaster basins provide indirect lighting and illuminate the ceiling mosaics. In the stair hall, on landings that lead up to the second-floor offices, are large, arched, leaded-glass windows. (The children's room, bindery, newspaper room, and applied science room were located on the ground floor.) The delivery hall, a large marble room lit by high arched windows, is connected to the reference room and the open shelf room on the exterior square, and to the main stack room through offices. A ceiling of dull gold molded plaster and slightly yellow window glass gave the room a warm glow. The rather plain reference and open shelf rooms to the west and east of the delivery hall are distinguished by exposed decorated ceiling beams.

In comparison to the Boston Public Library's centrally located reading room, the St. Louis Public Library functions better because delivery of books was given priority. Gilbert's large delivery hall is also easy to locate as the central focus, literally and figuratively, for the library building. Tucked in next to the main stack room on either side were elevators that accommodated the pulling, sorting, and delivery of books, using ground-floor areas. A seven-story steel-and-glass stack wing took up the entire north side of the library square (fig. 78). Storage and shipping rooms, as well as mechanical equipment, were located in the basement.[50]

Gilbert wanted to remind visitors of a certain period, namely the Renaissance, when learning was valued.[51] In the art collection, on the main floor and to the left as visitors entered, the ceiling was adapted from the Badia in Fiesole, built by Arnolfo di Cambio in 1285 and restored by Segaloni in 1625. Across the entry hall, in the periodical room, the ceiling was based on a study of the Laurentian Library in Florence, built from Michelangelo's designs between 1524 and 1571.[52] The scale of these rooms is quite different, but the overall mood was meant to echo the Renaissance effect of subdued grandeur.

Before the St. Louis Public Library opened, Gilbert had already received the commissions for two other libraries: one on the campus of the University of Texas at Austin (1909–11) and the other for the Ives Memorial Library (1908–11) in New Haven, Connecticut. The Building Committee of the Regents of the University of Texas appointed Gilbert architect for the university in January 1910 and accepted his design for a library (pl. 20). As university architect, Gilbert proposed several master campus plans, but he only executed two buildings, the library, now known as Battle Hall, and the Education Building (1915–18), now called Sutton Hall.[53] Gilbert's campus scheme would have created quadrangles with arcaded walkways between buildings (fig. 79).

The much-needed new library was finished by 1911 (fig. 80). With this project, Gilbert continued the exploration of Mediterranean Revival styles seen earlier in

78. St. Louis Public Library. Photograph c.1927 of stack side. St. Louis Public Library Archives.

79. Cass Gilbert, pencil sketch dated February 15, 1909, of Mediterranean-style buildings linked by arcaded walkways for the University of Texas, Austin, Texas. Cass Gilbert Collection, Prints and Photographs Division, Library of Congress.

80. Cass Gilbert, University of Texas Library (now called Battle Hall), Austin, Texas, 1909–11. New-York Historical Society.

81. University of Texas Library (now called Battle Hall). View of reading room. New-York Historical Society.

a small way in his court of the Art Building for the Louisiana Purchase Exposition.[54] The massing, however, is not much different from that of the Boston Public Library. At both libraries, the main floor is on the second level, following the prototype of the Italian *palazzo*. Texas limestone, polychrome terra cotta in the window surrounds, and carved brackets underneath the eaves add a richness that the McKim, Mead and White library lacked. Some Spanish elements of Texan heritage are recalled in the ironwork on exterior balconies and lanterns as well as inside in the stair hall. On the library's second floor, a domed rotunda opens into a large reading room lit by the tall, arched windows along the eastern facade and at the north and south ends. King-post trusses and carved wooden grilles in the interior have Spanish antccccdents as well[55] (fig. 81).

Gilbert's other building on the Austin campus, Sutton Hall (1915–18), shares certain characteristics with the library: a hipped roof in red tile, broad eaves, a main floor raised on a podium, and ample terra-cotta decoration (fig. 82). In the case of Sutton Hall, however, the ground floor is of smooth stone and the upper two floors are done in brick.

In 1913 Detroit held a competition for its municipal public library.[56] As Elizabeth Grossman aptly noted about the Detroit program: "The central question was whether the delivery room—where books were delivered to the reader and checked out—should by this date take architectural precedence over the

reading room, which had traditionally been both the grandest room in a library and the source of its characteristic windowed facade."[57] Gilbert had already answered that question in St. Louis with his delivery hall at the center, although it was not visible on the exterior. Detroit's needs were nearly identical to those of St. Louis. The three jurors selected Gilbert's plan and Renaissance Revival design (1913–21; fig. 83), which differed only slightly from his solution in St. Louis. While the jury was decisive about its preferences, the city of Detroit was plagued with financial problems that slowed construction considerably. Commissioned in 1913, the library opened only in 1921.

In Gilbert's winning scheme, all the main service areas were on the second level. Rather than two specialized reading rooms (art and periodicals) as he had provided in St. Louis, there were three general reading rooms behind an arcade. In Detroit, the arcaded loggia acted as a screen at the same time as it revealed the dimensions of the delivery room on the interior[58] (fig. 84).

Gilbert contributed one other monument to Detroit, on Belle Isle in the Detroit River between Lake St. Clair and Lake Erie. In 1914 he entered and won a competition for the design of the James Scott Memorial Fountain[59] (1921–22; pl. 21). Gilbert's ideas for the fountain were more ambitious than the James Scott bequest could underwrite, comprising landfill for additional park space, with an amphitheater and statue, and a lagoon. He also offered suggestions about a new bridge to Belle Isle.[60] By 1917, work had begun on the landfill; it was not until 1921 that construction of the scaled-back fountain began. While the white marble fountain was completed the following year (fig. 85), Gilbert's designs for landscaping and ancillary structures were never executed.

Gilbert's work in Oberlin, New Haven, Austin, and Detroit, was, in each case, to be part of a whole that he had also had a hand in planning. As with most large planning efforts, as time passed, funds dwindled or priorities shifted, and the whole remained a fragment. Nevertheless, Gilbert's partially completed schemes expanded his repertory of building types as well as the geographical reach of his practice. The museums, railroad stations, libraries, and educational buildings that resulted have now become part of the historic fabric of their areas, adapted and sometimes enlarged to suit the changing needs of their owners. The good survival rate of Gilbert's buildings is partly due to luck, but, to his credit, one or more aspects of his original buildings—the scale, decoration, placement of the building on the site, or interior volumes—have created sufficient respect or affection on the part of the owners to prompt them to find ways to keep the structures viable.

83. Cass Gilbert, Detroit Public Library, Detroit, Michigan, 1913–21. Floor plans. American Architect and Building News.

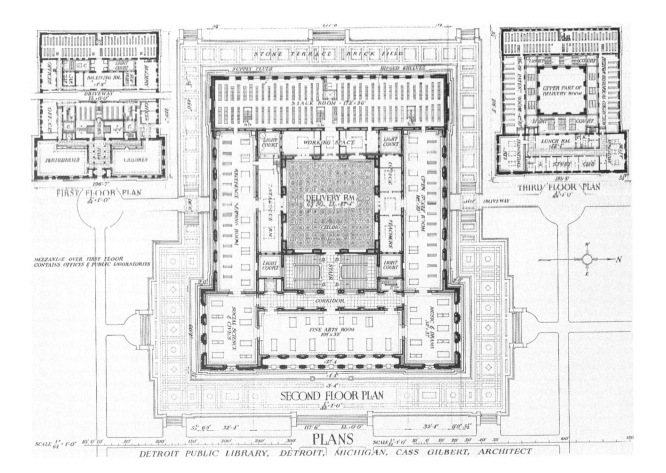

DETROIT PUBLIC LIBRARY, DETROIT, MICHIGAN, CASS GILBERT, ARCHITECT

110

84. Detroit Public Library. Facade. Courtesy of the Burton Historical Collection of the Detroit Public Library.

112

*85. Cass Gilbert,
James Scott Memo-
rial Fountain,
Belle Isle, Detroit,
Michigan, 1921–22.
Courtesy of the Bur-
ton Historical Collec-
tion of the Detroit
Public Library.*

BALANCING ACT
Commercial Heights and Civic Monumentality

A t the same time that Gilbert's practice was growing across the nation, the projects that significantly increased his professional prominence and financial status were in New York City. His designs for tall buildings—the West Street, Woolworth, and New York Life Insurance Company Buildings—were major contributions to a major metropolis. While they literally and figuratively rise above many architectural designs, for Gilbert they remained just one side of his design efforts. The other side, that of his institutional and monumental work, continued to occupy and, perhaps, balance his thinking. In this balancing act, private speculative office buildings became public monuments, and the organization and construction of public monuments benefited from lessons learned in tall office building design.

Designing tall required working closely with owner(s), financiers (often a group of investors), foundation and structural engineers, general contractors, real-estate agents, and other consultants. These individuals were sometimes at odds, and the fact that buildings were built at all is evidence of a collective determination to turn a profit and reshape the city. Gilbert's West Street Building (1905–7) in lower Manhattan, for example, took many forms before its twenty-three-story, U-shaped structure rose facing the Hudson River (fig. 86). Early schemes for the West Street Building featured a five-story tower. Some proposals were in a Romanesque Revival mode, others in Gothic (pl. 22; fig. 87), and yet another resembled Louis Sullivan's Wainwright Building (St. Louis, 1892). The tower was eventually eliminated, and Gilbert's office began revising the design, shifting away from the Romanesque to a flamboyant northern Gothic (fig. 88). Once the exterior scheme was resolved, the problem of building on a waterlogged site had to be addressed. After a bit of controversy, it was decided to use wood piles to support the structure.[1]

86. Cass Gilbert, West Street Building, New York City, 1905–7. New-York Historical Society, Irving Underhill, photographer.

87. West Street Building. Pencil sketch with tower, May 7, 1905. New-York Historical Society.

88. West Street Building. Sketch on tracing paper without tower. New-York Historical Society.

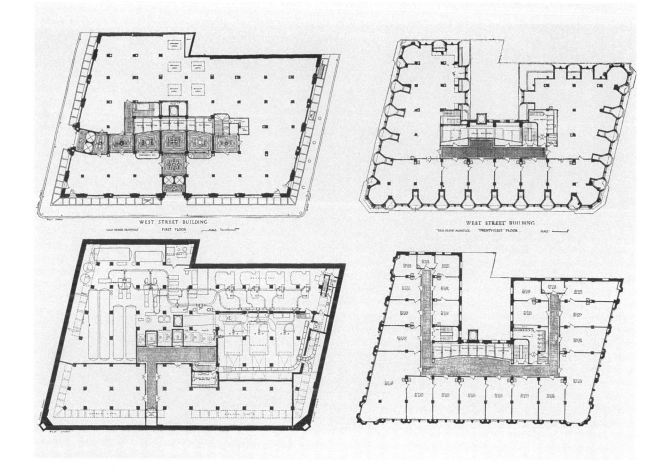

WEST STREET BUILDING
CASS GILBERT ARCHITECT   FIRST FLOOR   SCALE

WEST STREET BUILDING
CASS GILBERT ARCHITECT   TWENTY-FIRST FLOOR   SCALE

*89. West Street
Building. Plans.*
American Archi-
tect and Building
News.

*90. West Street
Building. Section
and rear view of
original scheme.*
American Archi-
tect and Building
News.

Gilbert's contributions to the West Street Building project went beyond
the important one of coordinating the various parties involved. The facade
designs and the building plan reveal his interest in pleasing the client by
creating a money-making structure. Profitability meant providing well-lit
office spaces that could be adapted for various kinds of tenants, speedy vertical transportation, an up-to-date physical plant, and a distinctive exterior
that captured attention. Perhaps inspired by the Dutch background of the
West Street Building's client and the Dutch history of Manhattan itself,
Gilbert's design team settled on thin vertical moldings of terra cotta that
drew the eye upward to ornament inspired by late medieval town and guild
halls of the Low Countries.[2] The client, Howard Carroll (1854–1916), was
vice president of the Starin Transportation Company. Carroll's father-in-law,
John Starin, was a prominent businessman of Dutch ancestry.[3] This investment building, then, while turning a profit, also celebrated personal and
municipal histories.

The ground floor was given over to elevators and the lobby, which had groin-
vaulted entrance halls (fig. 89). Here Gilbert collaborated for the first time
with the decorating firm of Paris and Wiley. These designers worked with him

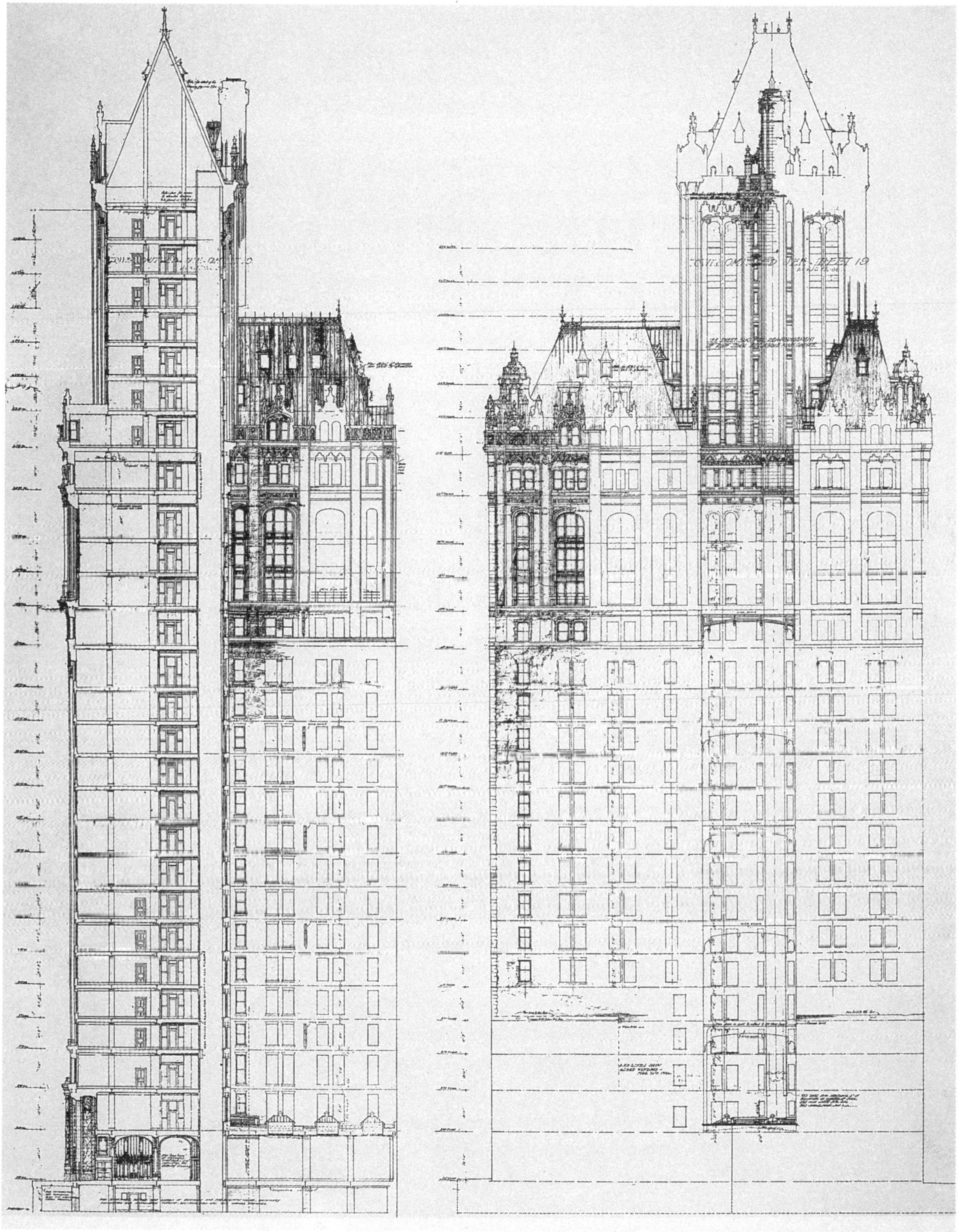

until the end of his career on projects that included the Detroit Public
Library and the United States Supreme Court building. For the West Street
Building, Francklyn Paris designed Gothic-inspired elevator screens, light fixtures, and stencil work for the vaults.[4] Offices wrap around a rear light court
on the oddly shaped site, with tie arches across the court adding interest to
the rear[5] (fig. 90).

Clearly other tall buildings were on Gilbert's mind as he designed the
West Street Building. The twenty-three-story Flatiron Building (1903) in
New York City by D. H. Burnham and Company was drawn in next to a
quick sketch of the West Street scheme (fig. 91). The tower makes
Gilbert's building taller, and the site makes it wider than the triangular
Flatiron. When Howard Carroll eliminated the tower, Gilbert's firm
reshaped the crown so that it would still capture the eye from the New
Jersey shore.[6] Gilbert's ambitions in 1905, perhaps frustrated after the
elimination of the West Street tower, were directed toward a fantasy
building 150 stories tall (fig. 92).

A 150 Story office Bldg
May 24, 1905

As the scale of skyscraper projects increased, so too did the attention they received from both the lay public and professionals. By 1910, Cass Gilbert had been involved with large-scale state and federal government projects as well as tall office buildings, but the stakes were raised with the commission for the Woolworth Company Building in New York, which he received in 1910 (fig. 93). While the Woolworth project presented many challenges unique to its client, its site, and its size, it shared features with other tall buildings, even moderately tall structures like Gilbert's own West Street Building.[7] Both the Woolworth and the West Street Buildings, for example, were designed to compete in the speculative real-estate market using eye-catching silhouettes and Gothic motifs. Facing City Hall Park and occupying the entire block between Park Place and Barclay Street on Broadway, the Woolworth Building was visible from many locations in Manhattan.

93. Cass Gilbert, F. W. Woolworth Company Building, New York City, 1910–13. New-York Historical Society.

Frank W. Woolworth (1852–1919) first contacted Cass Gilbert about an office building for his company headquarters in 1910. Woolworth headed an expanding retail enterprise, where items in his chain of stores typically sold for five or ten cents.[8] Unlike the West Street Building, which diminished in size as time proceeded, the Woolworth scheme grew and grew.[9] Gilbert's associate Thomas R. Johnson commemorated the main players in sculpted portraits on the entry level. Gilbert is depicted holding a model of the Woolworth Company Building (fig. 133). Louis Pierson grips a safe-deposit box in his capacity of president of the Irving Bank. Louis Horowitz of the Thompson-Starrett Company, the firm that won the construction contract, is shown talking on the telephone. Gunvald Aus, the structural engineer, holds a steel beam. The rental agent, Edward J. Hogan, holds a plan of the building. Frank Woolworth displays his nickels and dimes. Woolworth paid $13,500,000 in cash for his corporate headquarters.

One early, undated sketch for the Woolworth Building from the architect's sketchbook shows Gilbert's treatment of the base and the tower for an eighty foot frontage (fig. 94). The base of four bays looks similar to that of the West Street Building; the three-bay tower uses arcades to unite the upper stories. On April 25, 1910, Thomas R. Johnson completed a perspective study that developed ideas from the sketchbook, adding detail to the upper stages of the tower and broadening the base (pl. 23). Another Johnson drawing from July 1910 sets off the tower from the lower block on three sides and emphasizes its height with pronounced moldings (fig. 95). By December 31, 1910, a Gilbert study shows a four-bay lower block supporting a higher tower with several stages (fig. 96). Once the general proportions were decided, many studies were done to explore the most effective means to convey the "grand flying upwards" that Gilbert so admired in flamboyant Gothic buildings.[10] A Johnson study with traces of orange and blue proposes a design for the Woolworth Building crown, for example (fig. 97).

Frank Woolworth wanted an ostentatious building that would show off his fortune, but he recognized that the ostentation would have to pay off as well.

124

80'

Early study for
Woolworth Bldg

94 (opposite). F. W. Woolworth Company Building. Early pencil study with eighty-foot frontage. Sketchbook, Cass Gilbert Collection, Archives Center, National Museum of American History, Smithsonian Institution.

95. F. W. Woolworth Company Building. "Scheme 26" by Thomas R. Johnson, July 6, 1910. New-York Historical Society.

*96. F. W. Wool-
worth Company
Building. Study
by Cass Gilbert,
December 31,
1910. Cass Gilbert
Collection, Prints
and Photographs
Division, Library
of Congress.*

*97. F. W. Wool-
worth Company
Building. Sketch
of roof and lantern
of tower by Thomas
R. Johnson, Sep-
tember 28, 1911.
New-York Histori-
cal Society.*

Roof & Lantern of Tower
Woolworth Bldg
Cass Gilbert Architect

The Woolworth Building was both a speculative office building and a corporate headquarters.[11] Woolworth's firm occupied less than two floors of the building; the rest of the space was rented to much smaller firms, with the exception of the Irving National Bank, which occupied the first four floors and had been involved in the building scheme from its inception. The Woolworth Building's location, near the Manhattan terminus of the Brooklyn Bridge and fronting City Hall Park, was superb. Completed before World War I and the building boom of the 1920s, the Woolworth Building dominated the skyline for a decade and a half.

Because the Woolworth Building was the tallest building in the world from 1913 until 1930, it has received the most attention of all of Gilbert's designs.[12] When the building was completed, President Woodrow Wilson flipped a switch at the dedication that illuminated all fifty-five stories, 775 feet from street level to lantern top. The plan of the first floor encouraged passersby to enter one of the three main doors and proceed to a cross-shaped arcade featuring shops in an elegant interior of marble and mosaic (pl. 24; figs. 99 and 100). The Woolworth Building's steel frame was sheathed in cream-colored terra cotta molded into clustered columns, buttresses, gargoyles, crockets, and finials inspired by Gothic civic and ecclesiastical buildings of northern Europe;[13] Gilbert had looked to Low Country models for the West Street Building as well. The overall massing of the Woolworth Building includes a lower office block in a U shape around a light court—again, like the West Street Building—and then a central tower rising twenty-four stories above the block (figs. 98 and 101).

Undertaking this construction in 1911 required sinking sixty-nine pneumatic caissons to bedrock situated 100 to 120 feet below grade (fig. 102). The Foundation Company, the contractor for the substructure, excavated sixty thousand cubic yards of material. Since Woolworth wanted the building to be at least fifty feet higher than the Metropolitan Life Tower (1907–9), engineer Stephen F. Holtzman, who worked for the firm of Gunvald Aus and Co., determined what combination of steel columns, beams, gusset plates, braces, and trusses would keep such a high frame rigid against the wind[14] (fig. 103). Erection of the steel began on July 20, 1911.[15] The riveted frame was complete by June 30, 1912. Securing the terra cotta firmly in place was yet another challenge.[16] Plumbing, wiring, ventilating, and heating the tallest building in the world required innovative planning as well. Pipes and tanks, for example, were housed in low-head, unrentable stories between office floors.

Always meticulous, Gilbert lavished his attention on the shades and shapes of the terra-cotta ornament, the profiles of the building from up close as well as from a distance, the color schemes, and circulation patterns both outside and inside. The massing and the ornament attracted a diverse audience, both in New York and nationwide, which in turn gave an advantage to the Woolworth Company.[17] The Woolworth project brought Gilbert to international fame. He went from having a career as a successful designer of public and commercial

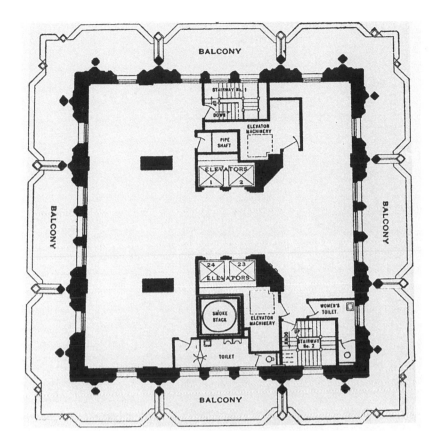

98. F. W. Woolworth Company Building. Forty-second-floor plan. American Architect and Building News.

99. F. W. Woolworth Company Building. Ground-floor plan. American Architect and Building News.

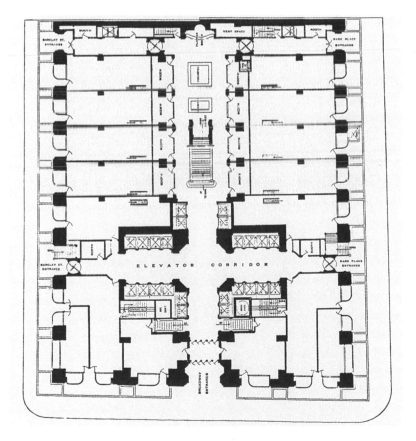

100 (opposite). F. W. Woolworth Company Building. Lobby. New-York Historical Society.

101. F. W. Woolworth Company Building. Rear (west) view. New-York Historical Society.

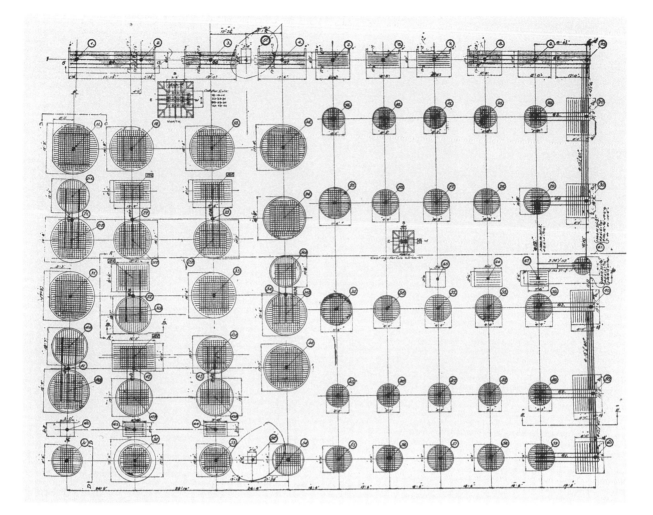

102. F. W. Wool-
worth Company
Building. Grillage
plan. American
Architect and
Building News.

structures to being a leader in architecture until the end of his life. While he
disliked some of the publicity his Woolworth design generated—particularly
the "cathedral of commerce" label—he benefited enormously from the
prestige it brought him.[18]

Despite being a private real-estate venture, the Woolworth Company Building
became a civic monument due to its height, its ornamentation, and its location. The building's public role had several aspects: as an advertising image, as
a site for entertainment and consumption, and as a feature on the skyline. Mil-
lions of people had emigrated to the United States by 1910, including nine
million between 1880 and 1900; another twelve million would arrive by 1914.
After 1890, many of those people came from eastern and southern Europe to
seek work in urban centers.[19] Men like Frank Woolworth recognized that these
people could become consumers of his dry goods. One way to welcome them
into the American economy and get them to shop at relatively new discount
chain stores was to establish a recognizable corporate symbol, such as the
Woolworth Building itself.[20] People become assimilated in a culture by finding
ways to fit in, through dress, food, and other preferences. Consumers could

buy Woolworth's products, needlebooks for a sewing kit, for example, identified by the corporate symbol, and be like many other Americans (fig. 104).

Further, the Woolworth Building offered the public a large lobby with shops and restaurants as well as elaborate decoration. The comparatively cramped entry area of a speculative office building like the West Street Building was expanded in the Woolworth Building to become a public space in a privately owned structure. People could buy entertainment there too, by purchasing tickets to the fifty-eighth-floor observatory. Many of the details on the building's exterior are entertaining. There are representations of bats, frogs, pelicans, pumas, owls, and a variety of human heads. The sculpted human heads, which seem to contemplate the pedestrians below, encircle the building (fig. 105). They give form to a widespread interest in America during the early twentieth century in categorizing humans according to so-called racial types. Earlier architectural manifestations of this interest are evident on the Library of Congress building (1886–97) in Washington, D.C., by Smithmeyer and Pelz, and on Gilbert's own United States Custom House.[21]

103. F. W. Woolworth Company Building. Portal arches and K-trusses for wind bracing. American Architect and Building News.

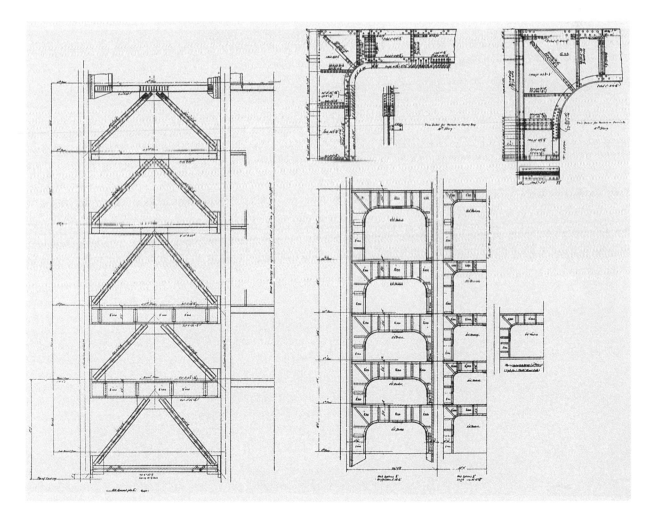

104. F. W. Wool-
worth Company
Building. Needle-
book with corporate
office building.
Collection of the
author.

105. F. W. Wool-
worth Company
Building. New
York City. Sculpted
head. Photograph
by the author.

Another way to gain public favor for those traveling to and from New York
(by boat) was to design a tower that rose above its neighbors but still fit in.
On the skyline, the Woolworth Building stands out clearly, but the tower is set
back from a cornice line at the rear that respects the height of other nearby
buildings.[22] Despite the greatly increased scale of the Woolworth Building in
contrast to the West Street Building, both structures share Gilbert's use of picturesque eclecticism to enhance his client's real-estate income as well as the
urban landscape. Muralist Edwin Blashfield, a friend of Gilbert's, remarked in
1907: "I want to write a line to tell you what a splendid impression your West
Street Building makes on one, as one comes up the harbor on the way back
from the other side of the Atlantic . . . Indeed I didn't suppose a skyscraper
could be so picturesque and handsome."[23] In 1913, when Gilbert sketched the
silhouette of Durham Cathedral from below the cliffs, he was painting what
he sought to create at home: a romantic vision that captured people's imagi-
nations as well as their wallets[24] (pl. 18). In describing his tour of English
cathedrals in 1906, Gilbert wrote to his wife:

> York repeated our experience at Peterborough and Lincoln and Ely in
> our approach to it. It is . . . the feature of this trip to have seen . . . these
> great structures rise at a distance of five miles or more to gradually develop
> clearer . . . as we approached . . . It was as the great architects who may
> have designed them would probably have chosen to study them: first in the
> mass and in silhouette, then little by little in composition and perspective

in slowly dawning solids and voids of wall surface and finally in the full splendor of their marvelous and complicated forms and exuberant detail.[25] The Woolworth Building is more than just a technical triumph, a formal success, or an organizational feat. Its architecture fostered an ordered, profitable system that, to an extent, assimilated various ethnic groups. Its scale and popular imagery distinguished it as a public landmark until at least 1930.

While the Woolworth Building design was underway, Gilbert teamed up with the Cincinnati firm of Garber and Woodward to design the thirty-four-story Union Central Life Insurance Company Building (1911–13; now called Central Trust Tower; fig. 106) in Cincinnati. When it was completed, it was the fifth tallest building in the world and Cincinnati's tallest until 1930.[26] The exterior of the tower is clad in white terra cotta, but that is where its similarity to the Woolworth Building in New York ends. There is none of the flame-like verticality of the Woolworth Building. The upper Ionic colonnade and pyramidal roof in fact bear some resemblance to the Hellenistic tomb of King Mausolus at Halicarnassus. The small lantern hides a smokestack. While not a remarkable Gilbert building except in scale, the Union Central Building shows the range of his work and the various solutions he could propose simultaneously.

The composition of the Union Central Building was revisited even less successfully at the end of Gilbert's career, in the bulky Federal Courthouse (1929–36) at Foley Square in New York City (fig. 107). Here, the tower was reduced to twenty stories and set atop a five-story block at the base. This solution provided offices and even a rifle range for a wide variety of law-enforcement-related activities, but the exterior massing and classical grandeur do little more than dwarf the visitor.[27]

Building for the government or for institutions was often slow in contrast to the rapid construction of commercial structures for investors who sought to turn a profit as quickly as possible. One government project that Gilbert and his team designed and executed in record time was the United States Military Ocean Terminal (1918–19) in Brooklyn, New York. This complex of warehouses, power plant, administration building, and docks was a testimony to Gilbert's planning abilities as well as to his design sense. The Austin, Nichols and Company Warehouse complex (1909–23) that Gilbert designed in Brooklyn had given him some prior experience with industrial projects (pl. 25; figs. 108 and 109).

The American entry into World War I on April 6, 1917, brought about a restructuring of military personnel and necessitated, among other efforts, the development of efficient systems for loading, unloading, and storing matériel and housing and transporting troops.[28] To that end, large-scale building projects were initiated and completed quickly, including Gilbert's Brooklyn Military Ocean Terminal, also called the Army Supply Base (fig. 110). The terminal was sited on the riverfront, adjacent to the Bay Ridge Terminal of the

*106. Cass Gilbert
with Garber and
Woodward, Union
Central Life Insur-
ance Company
Building (Central
Trust Tower),
Cincinnati, Ohio,
1911–13. Hugh-
son Hawley render-
ing. New-York His-
torical Society.*

107 (opposite).
Cass Gilbert,
Federal Courthouse,
Foley Square,
New York City,
1929–36. Prints
and Photographs
Division, Library
of Congress.

108 (above).
Cass Gilbert,
Austin, Nichols
and Company
Warehouse, Brook-
lyn, New York City,
1909–23. New-
York Historical
Society.

109. Austin,
Nichols and Com-
pany Warehouse.
New-York Histori-
cal Society.

110. Cass Gilbert, United States Military Ocean Terminal (Army Supply Base), Brooklyn, New York City, 1918–19. New-York Historical Society.

Long Island and Pennsylvania railroads; there were also direct rail lines to the New York, New Haven and Hartford line over the Hell Gate Bridge. The Brooklyn complex was designed to utilize a combination of rail, lighter, and car ferry to transfer goods.[29]

At the Brooklyn Military Ocean Terminal, the four piers averaged 1,300 feet long, providing berths for ocean-going ships (fig. 112). The piers were two-tiered steel structures with timber roofs, reinforced-concrete slab floors, and vertically movable doors in the bays (fig. 111). Gilbert designed two eight-story concrete warehouses linked to the piers and to each other that were at that time the largest structures ever built of reinforced concrete[30] (fig. 113). The Brooklyn project was conceived to fill an immediate need, and reinforced concrete met both the criteria of speed of execution and of minimal usage of steel, which was scarce at the time. The thirty-five-million-dollar complex was built in less than a year, with the piers and buildings in use within six months.[31]

Early sketches on yellow legal paper show Gilbert's focus on the relationship between the warehouse blocks and the piers. For example, a sketch dated February 4, 1918, clearly delineates a connection between the three closed piers and the smaller warehouse, and then with the bridges between the two warehouses (fig. 114). Rail lines have also been sketched in. Another sketch shows a similar connection among the piers and warehouses, but the larger warehouse is organized around four courtyards. This scheme was rejected. Instead, what became known as Warehouse B is distinguished by the 66-foot-wide interior court that runs 740 feet through the building's length, with rail lines coming right into it (fig. 115). Staggered receiving balconies cantilever out into the glass-covered atrium. This solution was derived from Albert Kahn and Ernest Wilby's design for the Ford Motor Company plant annex (1918) at Highland Park, Michigan, just outside Detroit, having been suggested to Gilbert by a superintendent of the Ford Company, C. W. Avery[32] (fig. 116).

Albert Kahn (in association with Ernest Wilby from 1902 to 1918) had been designing for the automobile industry in Detroit from the start of his practice in 1895.[33] He was assisted in the design of industrial buildings by his engineer brother, Julius Kahn. Henry Ford's ideas about labor management and mass production dovetailed with the Kahn brothers' engineering and design to produce flexible, efficient manufacturing spaces. Moritz Kahn, the third brother involved with designing for the automobile industry, wrote in his book, *The Design and Construction of Industrial Buildings:* "With the simplest materials and the simplest forms of treatment a capable architect can produce pleasing results."[34] He might have written the same about Gilbert's Brooklyn Military Terminal.[35]

The Military Ocean Terminal was designed to transfer goods from ship to warehouse to rail and back again—not, of course, to design cars. Freight could be brought right into the warehouse atrium and loaded or unloaded

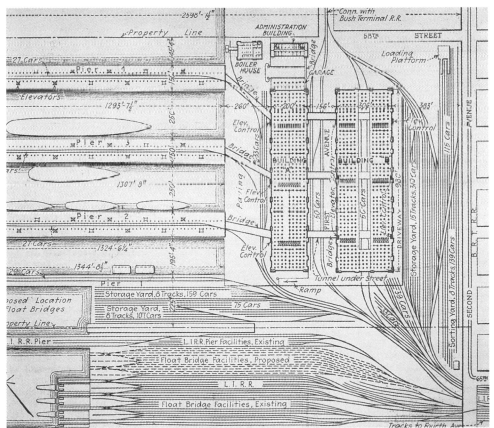

111. United States Military Ocean Terminal (Army Supply Base). Second deck of pier. Architectural Review.

112. United States Military Ocean Terminal (Army Supply Base). Plan. American Architect.

113. United States
Military Ocean
Terminal (Army
Supply Base).
Rendering of bridge
between powerhouse
and warehouse.
New-York Histori-
cal Society.

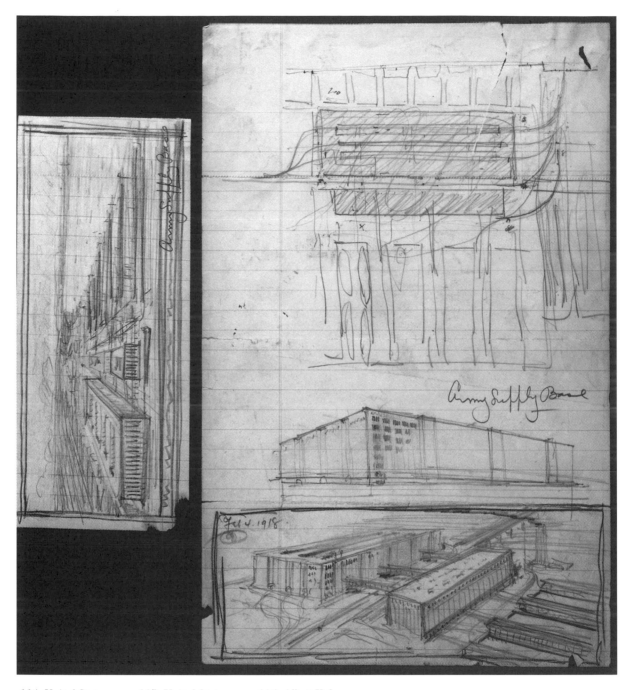

114. United States Military Ocean Terminal (Army Supply Base). Sketch on legal paper, February 4, 1918. Cass Gilbert Collection, Archives Center, National Museum of American History, Smithsonian Institution.

115. United States Military Ocean Terminal (Army Supply Base). Interior of Warehouse B. Photograph by Pamela Hepburn.

116. Albert Kahn with Ernest Wilby, Ford Motor Company plant annex, 1918, Highland Park, Michigan. Interior. New-York Historical Society.

at all levels using electric traveling cranes that were suspended from the roof. The warehouses and piers were connected by subterranean tunnels and by bridges on the third floor. The supply terminal featured the largest installation of Otis elevators to that date—ninety-six of them. These were operated on prearranged schedules by dispatchers at centrally located service banks. The elevators featured an early version of the automatic leveling device.

The Henry C. Turner Construction Company had specialized in industrial construction using reinforced concrete since 1902.[36] At the Brooklyn terminal, the Turner Company employed Claude Allen Porter Turner's patented system of spirally reinforced concrete columns. C. A. P. Turner had developed this concrete-column-and-slab construction system in 1905 and patented it in 1908.[37] The three-foot-diameter columns were spaced twenty feet apart on centers and supported girderless concrete slabs[38] (fig. 117).

The exterior of each warehouse was organized into vertical bays with mullions breaking up the massive bulk of the buildings (fig. 118). Concrete sections marked a rhythm, projecting out every two bays, then four bays, then two bays again. The concrete projections, which contained elevators, stairs, or toilets, also emphasized the articulation of the corners. The facades clearly revealed the vertical circulation patterns and the acres of open storage space inside.

The Brooklyn terminal was an anomaly in Gilbert's career. The decision to use concrete was a direct response to a functional need rather than the result of any formal or stylistic considerations.[39] In a draft of an article, Gilbert wrote that the supply terminal "is of an extremely practical character demonstrating that ornamental detail is not necessarily a feature of architectural design where vast spaces predominate. In fact, ornament of any kind would seem flippant and trivial in so great and impressive a mass."[40] When building

117. United States Military Ocean Terminal (Army Supply Base). Interior columns in Warehouse B. Photograph by the author.

118. United States Military Ocean Terminal (Army Supply Base). Exterior of Warehouse B. New-York Historical Society.

program and economic conditions permitted it, however, Gilbert used ornament in his large-scale designs.

After World War I, Cass Gilbert's private architectural commissions continued to be so large in scale that they had a public role in their urban setting. The Woolworth Building had altered the urban landscape of New York City because of its height, its careful detailing, and its entertainment value. It culminated an era of technical and artistic exploration of skyscraper design at the same time that it introduced another era: that of the commercial use of skyscrapers for corporate imaging purposes. Never before the Woolworth

119. Cass Gilbert, New York Life Insurance Company Building, New York City, 1925–28. Prints and Photographs Division, Library of Congress.

New York Life is large, conservative, and dull. Reassuring in times like these, isn't it?

120. New York Life Insurance Company Building. Advertisement for New York Life Insurance Company, 1990. With permission of New York Life Insurance Company.

Building had a private investment served to such an extent as a public commodity. By the time Gilbert's firm designed the New York Life Insurance Company Building, built between 1925 and 1928, the corporate use of a building to represent its public image was well established.

In contrast to the lacy, delicate, and gleaming tower that Gilbert had designed for Frank Woolworth, the New York Life Insurance Company Building on Madison Avenue between Twenty-sixth and Twenty-seventh Streets is formidable, dark, and staid (fig. 119). The predictability and dependability of its design were recognized as assets even in the last decade of the twentieth century, when it was used in a print advertisement for the company (fig. 120). Gothic details embellish the limestone, but they do not detract from the geometric setbacks.[41] While the Woolworth Building displays some whimsy, the New York Life Building offers few surprises.

McKim, Mead and White's Madison Square Garden was demolished to build Gilbert's New York Life Insurance Company Building.[42] The building's base occupied the site fully and then the volume was sliced dramatically to culminate in a gilded pinnacled roof above the tower stage. In a small December 1919 sketch for the New York Life Building, Gilbert made the tower seem

121. New York Life Insurance Company Building. Pencil sketch dated December 1919. Cass Gilbert Collection, Prints and Photographs Division, Library of Congress.

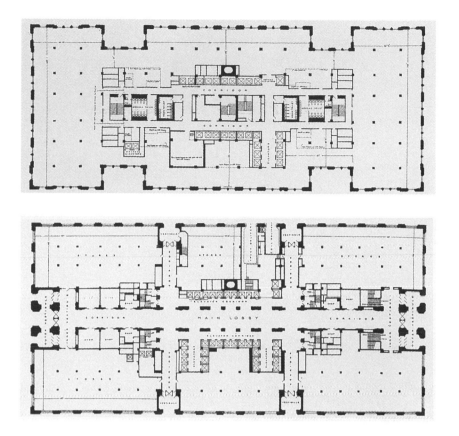

122. *New York Life Insurance Company Building. Plan for fifth to thirteenth floors.* American Architect.

123. *New York Life Insurance Company Building. First-floor plan.* American Architect.

more pronounced by taking a worm's-eye view and thrusting the lower wings out toward the viewer (fig. 121). In the built version, floor upon floor of rectangular windows draw the eye upward to spiky ornament at the cornice line. The building's decoration is a composite of Renaissance, Gothic, and Art Deco that Gilbert called "American Perpendicular," while the massing of the four main blocks that comprise the skyscraper shares the geometry of other tall buildings of the 1920s. The plan included public spaces on the first four floors and offices up to the thirtieth story for 3,500 employees of the life insurance company and other tenants[45] (figs. 122 and 123).

A central core contained all the utilities, with offices arranged around the exterior to receive maximum light and air. The interior spaces for the insurance company were designed to be homelike, based on eighteenth-century English precedents. The staff was divided by sex and rank with separate dining rooms for men and women, department heads and company officers. There were extensive medical facilities for company employees. This emphasis on healthful diet, preventive health care, and an uplifting atmosphere was viewed as a good business investment, especially for a company insuring health and life.

It seemed acceptable to many city dwellers who used the building or who passed by that the New York Life Insurance Company, a private corporation, had covered its steel-framed headquarters with carved limestone. When public

money was to be expended to cover the steel towers of the George Washington Bridge (1926–31) over the Hudson River, however, there was substantial public resistance. Cass Gilbert had been asked to design the approaches to and the cladding for the towers of Othmar Ammann's suspension bridge at 178th Street; he offered numerous proposals for granite sheathing, in different historical styles (fig. 124). Gilbert's proposed treatments were all rejected. The *New York Times* editorialized in 1931 that the bridge remains "stark and unadorned . . . with a certain functional grace which makes a special appeal to the present generation."[44]

Traditional styles continued to appeal to many though. Gilbert received several commissions for buildings in Connecticut, where he had a country house. For most of these designs, he chose Georgian Revival styles, executed in brick or stone. Examples include the Ives Memorial Library in New Haven (see Chapter 3) and, in Waterbury, the Municipal Building (1914–15; fig. 125), offices for the Chase Manufacturing Company (1917–19; fig. 126), and the Waterbury Club[45] (1917–18; fig. 127). The brick Municipal Building and Waterbury Club are characterized by Georgian motifs much enlarged in scale. The Chase Manufacturing Company had been known since Colonial times for its watches and other brass products. It is fitting, therefore, that Gilbert again visited the Georgian style to present the Company's public image in this old Colonial town.[46]

Gilbert's Anglophilia never waned from his student days, although he never attempted an archaeological or strictly historical approach to his stylistic references.[47] By 1930, when he designed the New York County Lawyer's

124 (opposite). Cass Gilbert, stone and concrete cladding (unexecuted) for the George Washington Bridge over the Hudson River, New York–New Jersey, 1926–31. Charcoal sketch by J. T. Cronin, 1927. New York Historical Society.

125. Cass Gilbert, Municipal Building, Waterbury, Connecticut, 1914–15. American Architect and Building News.

Association, Gilbert chose to echo the Federal period in American architecture (and, indirectly, the work of Robert Adam) as well as London clubhouses (fig. 128). Gilbert's flat infill facade on Vesey Street in lower Manhattan is carefully proportioned and understated, providing a fitting backdrop for fine wrought-iron fencing and decoration.

If the New York Bar Association got a Georgian Federal clubhouse, what sort of building did the United States Supreme Court justices get? As early as 1927, Cass Gilbert was planning the first permanent building for the Supreme Court of the United States in Washington, D.C., which would be completed only in 1935, a year after his death[48] (fig. 129). While the New York Lawyer's Association design was private and modest in scale, the Supreme Court Building was a public monument for the highest legal appointees in the country on a site that had been selected in 1901 but was not acquired until 1926. Just as legal decisions are based on precedents, so too did Gilbert look to ancient Rome and Greece for precedents for his monumental

*129. Cass Gilbert,
United States
Supreme Court
Building, Wash-
ington, D.C.,
1928–35. Main
facade. Franz
Jantzen, photog-
rapher. Collection
of the Supreme
Court of the
United States.*

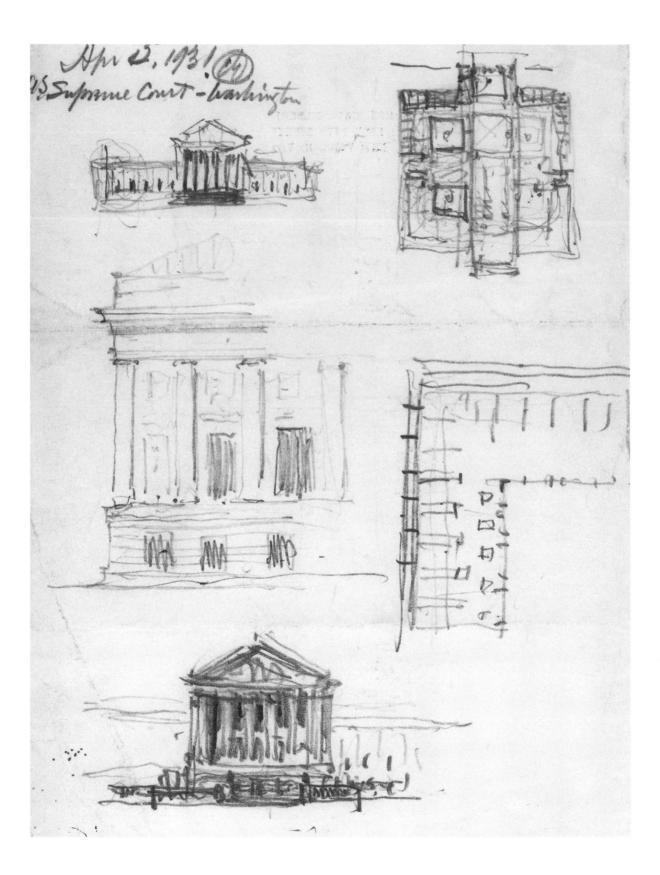

Apr 23, 1931 ㉔
U.S. Supreme Court - Washington

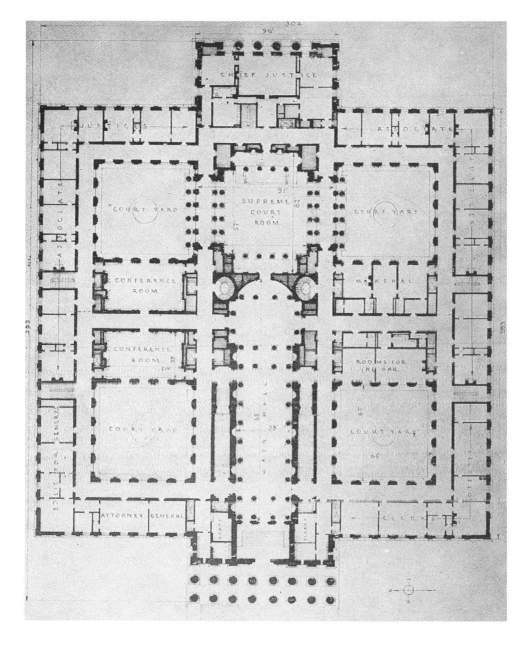

130 (opposite). United States Supreme Court Building. Pencil sketches of plans and elevations, April 5, 1931. Cass Gilbert Collection, Prints and Photographs Division, Library of Congress.

131. United States Supreme Court Building. Main-floor plan. Architecture.

scheme; he also consulted nineteenth-century French sources, among others.[49] A sketch from 1931 summarizes the building: a central temple front has recessed colonnaded wings with end pavilions on each side (fig. 130). An idealized temple seemed out of step to many during the Depression, but the Commission of Fine Arts and the federal government supported his design.[50] The judicial branch of government received a classicizing building consistent with the houses of Congress and the executive branch.

The Supreme Court Building has a double colonnade of eight columns that dwarfs the visitor. To each side, Gilbert placed lower wings whose walls are elaborated with Ionic pilasters and flanking windows. The contrast between the solidity and the smaller scale of the wings and the tall column-screened temple itself literally differentiates the functions of the building parts and underscores the ceremony of rising to meet the law. The desire to create a timeless, hierarchical structure may seem timebound in the late twentieth century, but Gilbert provided a superbly crafted monument for upholding what he viewed as the Western tradition.

For visitors, movement toward and into the Supreme Court Building is highly regulated and focused.[51] A short flight of steps leads to an expansive terrace; the temple is on a high podium across the terrace and at the top of the stairs. Passing through the portico of tightly and evenly spaced colossal Corinthian columns and beneath a coffered ceiling, the visitor finds the entrance (fig. 131). Once inside, Doric colonnades line the marble grand hall that leads to the Supreme Court Chamber. The chamber entrance is heralded by columns that define an anteroom. If the visitor had doubts that the decisions handed down here were weighty, this sequence of marble spaces would dispel them. The chamber itself, bounded on four sides by Ionic columns supporting an architrave and sculpted frieze, is both formal and forbidding.[52] Twin marble elliptical staircases flank the chamber and run from bottom to top of the central section of the building, recalling a circulation solution Gilbert had used in the Minnesota Capitol forty years earlier (fig. 132).

From the Minnesota State Capitol to the United States Supreme Court Building, from the Endicott Building to the New York Life Insurance Company Building, Gilbert's designs defined a continuum that extended in time for fifty years and crossed much of the United States. The coherence of Gilbert's designs derived from his lifelong commitment to traditional styles adapted to modern building techniques and functions. His monumental public work coexisted easily with his commercial designs, in part because of their large scale and the increasing similarities between the organization of business and government. American cities became more diverse in the late nineteenth and early twentieth centuries, and Gilbert's success can be measured by his talent for using architectural forms to connect disparate activities and people.

*132. United States
Supreme Court
Building. Interior
spiral stairs.
Collection of the
Supreme Court of
the United States.*

CONCLUSION

By the late 1920s, Cass Gilbert could look back on a long career in architecture. His letters indicate both the pleasure and the sorrow these memories brought, while a drawing of August 1928 reveals a certain pride in the "city" full of buildings he had designed (fig. 134). He had only once taken on a partner, confessing to Henry Rutgers Marshall an unwillingness to share the load.[1] As he noted in a 1927 letter to a former employee, E. S. J. Phillips, Ralph Waldo Emerson's essay on self-reliance "stuck with me all my life." He quoted Emerson: "Ask nothing of any man and in the endless mutation it must presently appear that thou only, firm column, are the supporter of all that surround thee!"[2] Despite Gilbert's self-image as a supporting column, he did recognize the contributions of others to his practice and his family's prosperity (fig. 133).

Content with his life and yet acknowledging his own limitations, Gilbert wrote to archaeologist Francis Bacon, a long-time friend, in 1927:

> We are just two old boys—Just as enthusiastic and idealistic as ever. Me—I am a little "liverey" now and then and sometimes a bit overworked, and not time enough in the 24 hours to do 26 hours of work in . . . A little bit more particular about matters of design—a little more convinced that a big plan and a big ensemble is [sic] more important than a quaint little mantelpiece or a newel post—but after all these are not matters of the heart or soul, and in the cosmos in which we live they are infinitesimal details. What irks me and rides me is a damnable sense of responsibility—It is an inheritance from my ancestors I think—Quakers-Puritans-Covenanters-Presbyterians and Crusaders. What a lot they must have been. And so I never have time to loaf with a friend when I know that my job is lagging behind: but must forsooth spur myself on to make good as best I can whatever I may have undertaken. My life was always like that. It always will be.[3]

133. Cass Gilbert, F. W. Woolworth Company Building, New York City, 1910–13. View of Cass Gilbert sculpture in elevator hall by Thomas R. Johnson. Photograph by Pamela Hepburn.

Gilbert lived, perhaps anachronistically, what Emerson had essayed: "The American who would serve his country must learn the beauty and honor of perseverance, he must reinforce himself by the power of character, and revisit the margin of that well from which his fathers drew waters of life and enthusiasm, the fountain I mean of the moral sentiments."[4] Gilbert's sense of responsibility led, more often than not, to excellent designs that were masterfully executed and pleasurable to behold in detail and massing. Frequently those designs drew on the heritage of "his fathers."[5] Gilbert sustained a remarkably consistent production of high-quality designs that met the needs and desires of a large number of clients across the United States. To do this, by his own account, he remained stubbornly independent, tethered to past traditions in the midst of a rapidly changing society.[6] This juxtaposition seemed to strengthen his sense of self at the same time that it helped shape American architecture.

166

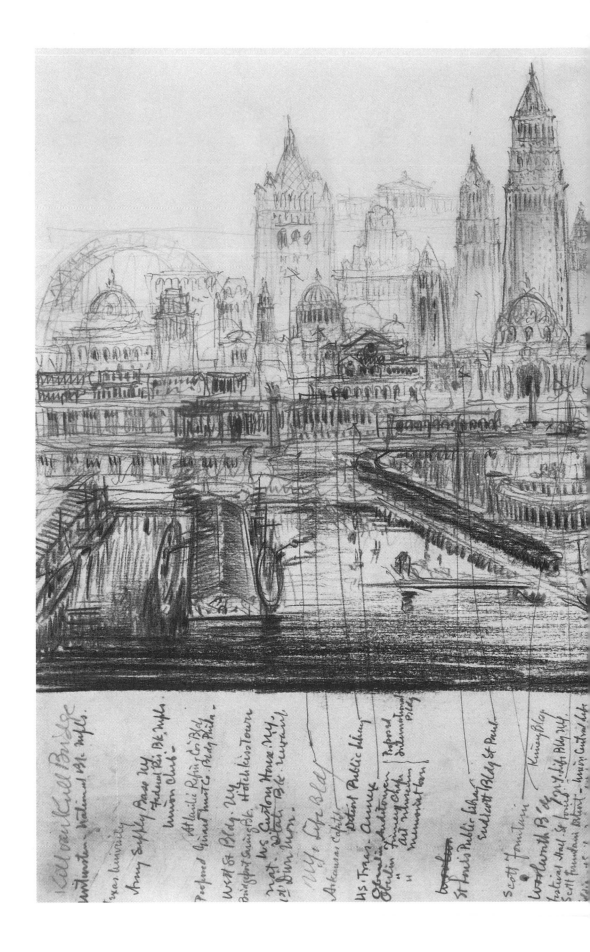

134. Cass Gilbert, drawing of many of the large projects developed during his career, August 1928. Prints and Photographs Division, Library of Congress.

ACKNOWLEDGMENTS

I was born seven years shy of one hundred years after Cass Gilbert's birth, in the same month. My parents are Quaker: Gilbert's mother supposedly was as well. Like Gilbert, I grew up in St. Paul, Minnesota, having also lived in Ohio. While my life has been considerably different from Gilbert's, I have felt a connection to him ever since I did an undergraduate project on the Woolworth Company Building in 1978. Our twenty-year relationship has been challenging and beneficial to me. My first acknowledgment is to him and his family for saving so much of his material. While at times the volume of documentation has been daunting, there is great reward for a scholar in finding answers that one is seeking in papers, drawings, and photographs.

The second acknowledgment is to my own family, to whom this book is dedicated. They made it possible to compose this book. Betty Irish, my mother, clipped newspapers, collected booklets, and toured houses with and for me until her death in 1985. Her joy in art and architecture has been an invaluable gift. Reed Larson, my husband, believed I could write this book and bolstered me. Our children, Miriam and Renner Larson, seem to have coped with a mother at the computer in the basement. All of my in-laws, my two sisters, and my father provided housing, food, and child care, not to mention what Gilbert would call an "esprit de corps."

It is a pleasure to acknowledge my other debts, which are numerous indeed after all these years. My friends in New York City who housed and fed me so many times prove how hospitable that city can be: Susan Ball and Ned Kaufman, Stan and Lyn Brooks, Pamela Hepburn, Mary Ellen Isaacs, and Sarah Landau. Susan Lorenz in St. Louis has been a wonderful hostess and friend over the years. Marilyn Booth, Nancy Crego, Kim Glenn, and Carol Spindel, writers and friends, have encouraged me many times. Betsy Grossman and Richard Chafee in Providence, Rhode Island, have been supportive and interested colleagues.

In graduate school, my professors, the late Bainbridge Bunting, the late Carl Condit, and David Van Zanten, provided helpful feedback, challenging questions, and substantive conversations from which I continue to benefit. Hard it is to thank people adequately for stirring an interest in me that became so central and important in my life. I am grateful to Professor Henry Binford for serving on my dissertation committee. Northwestern University's graduate dean Clarence Ver Steeg came through with money and moral support when I needed it.

The hard-working and talented staff members at the many institutions that house Gilbert's papers have been wonderful. The dedicated people at the New-York Historical Society have made my research possible all along: Mary Beth Betts and Wendy Shadwell have been indispensable; former Historical Society employees Nina Rutenberg Gray and Helena Zinkham also were helpful. Janet Parks, curator of drawings at the Avery Library at Columbia University, has made working at Columbia easy and always pleasant. The staff and resources at the Minnesota Historical Society are real treasures. The other institutions that I have visited and have been provided with welcome assistance include: in Washington, D.C., the Archives of the American Institute of Architects, the Library of Congress Manuscripts and Prints and Photographs Divisions, the National Archives and Records Administration, the National Museum of American Art and the National Museum of American History, and the Archives of the Supreme Court and United States Capitol; in New York, the National Academy of Design; in Newark, New Jersey, the Newark Public Library; in Oberlin, Ohio, the Allen Art Museum and the Oberlin College Archives; in St. Louis, the Missouri Historical Society, the St. Louis Art Museum, and the Archives of Washington University; in St. Paul, the J. J. Hill Reference Library and the Northwest Architectural Archives; and in Minneapolis, the University of Minnesota Archives at Walter Library.

I have relied extensively on the excellent library collections available where I have worked: the Northwestern University libraries in Evanston, Illinois, the Burnham Library of the Art Institute of Chicago, the Regenstein Library of the University of Chicago, and the libraries of the University of Illinois at Urbana-Champaign. The staff who augment and manage these collections deserve kudos.

Colleagues who have shared information, ideas, and interest for years are reason enough to spend time in mail rooms or slide libraries (or restaurants). These people include: Kathryn Anthony, Richard Betts, Robert Bruegmann, Walter Creese, Kathleen Roy Cummings, Joan Draper, John Garner, Dianne Harris, Kathleen James, Paul Kruty, Alan Lathrop, Katherine Manthorne, Anne Marshall, Barbara Mooney, Robert Mooney, Dale Mulfinger, Robert Ousterhout, Barry Riccio and Amita Sinha. Other scholars who have been following Cass Gilbert's trails have been companionable and generous: Gerald Baum, Geoffrey Blodgett, Gail Fenske, Philip Larson, William Towner Morgan, Patricia Murphy, Osmund Overby, and Michael Richman. Gail Fenske and Kim Glenn each read the entire penultimate draft of this book and gave me valuable feedback. Then Kim Glenn reread the revisions. Blessings on her. Denise Bratton was a thorough and conscientious editor.

Several people who have no apparent interest in Cass Gilbert but who have taught me much about how I might fit into architectural history also deserve thanks for the work they do: Jerri Allyn, Donna Henes, Jerry Kreiman, Suzanne Lacy, Sabra Moore, and Wabun-Inini.

The institutions that have provided me with welcome research funds include: Northwestern University (Dissertation Year Fellowship), the Howard Phalin Foundation for Graduate Study in Chicago, the J. J. Hill Reference Library, the Research Board of the University of Illinois at Urbana-Champaign, and the Minnesota Historical Society.

Finally, I am grateful to Robert A. M. Stern, The Monacelli Press, and my editor, Andrea Monfried, for the opportunity to write this monograph and select the illustrations of Gilbert's work.

NOTES

Primary materials in various collections have been indispensable for my research. The institutions are abbreviated in the notes as follows:

LofC: Library of Congress, Washington, D.C.
MHS: Minnesota Historical Society, St. Paul, Minnesota
MoHS: Missouri Historical Society, St. Louis, Missouri
NARA: National Archives and Records Administration, Washington, D.C.
NMAH: National Museum of American History, Smithsonian Institution, Washington, D.C.
N-YHS: New-York Historical Society, New York, New York
WNRC: Washington National Records Service, Suitland, Maryland

PREFACE

1. Igor Stravinsky, *Poetics of Music in the Form of Six Lessons,* trans. Arthur Knodel and Ingolf Dahl (New York: Vintage Books, 1947), 59.

INTRODUCTION

1. For histories of architectural training, consult among other sources, James Philip Noffsinger, *The Influence of the Ecole des Beaux-Arts on the Architects of the United States* (Washington, D.C.: Catholic University of America Press, 1955); Richard Oliver, *The Making of an Architect, 1881–1981* (New York: Rizzoli, 1981); Caroline Shillaber, *The Massachusetts Institute of Technology School of Architecture and Planning, 1861–1961: A Chronicle* (Cambridge, Mass.: M.I.T. Press, 1963); and Arthur C. Weatherhead, "The History of Collegiate Education in Architecture in the United States" (Ph.D. diss., Columbia University, New York, 1941).
2. For background information, see Thomas C. Cochran and William Miller, *The Age of Enterprise: A Social History of Industrial America,* rev. ed. (New York: Harper and Row, 1961); Edward C. Kirkland, *Dream and Thought in the Business Community, 1860–1900* (Chicago: Quadrangle Books, 1956); David Potter, *People of Plenty: Economic Abundance and the American Character* (Chicago: University of Chicago Press, 1954); and Alan Trachtenberg, *The Incorporation of America: Culture and Society in the Gilded Age* (New York: Hill and Wang, 1982).
3. See George Kubler on good and bad entrances, *The Shape of Time: Remarks on the History of Things* (New Haven: Yale University Press, 1962), 6.
4. 4. These Europeans were not often flattering in their comments, but they did take notice. On Gilbert's United States Custom House, for example, see Le Corbusier, *When the Cathedrals Were White,* trans. Francis E. Hyslop Jr. (New York: McGraw-Hill [1947], 1964), 60. Marcel Duchamp thought of the Woolworth Tower as a readymade. Craig Adcock, "Marcel Duchamp's Approach to New York: 'Find an Inscription for the Woolworth Building as a Readymade,'" *Dada/Surrealism* 14: 52–65. Thanks to Professor Jeffrey Howe of Boston College for his help. On Le Corbusier's and Neutra's use of images of the United States Military Ocean Terminal in Brooklyn, see Chapter 4, note 40.
5. William Hubbard's *Complicity and Conviction: Steps toward an Architecture of Convention* (Cambridge, Mass.: M.I.T. Press, 1980) is an excellent resource for thinking about architectural design. Other discussions about styles during the American Renaissance include Dwight James Baum, "Modern Traditionalism," *T-Square Club Journal of Philadelphia* 1 (January 1931): 14–15, 41–42; Sharon Irish, "Cass Gilbert's New York Career, 1899–1905" (Ph.D. diss., Northwestern University, Evanston, Ill., 1985), especially 11–18; and Robert A. M. Stern, Gregory Gilmartin, and John Massengale, *New York 1900: Metropolitan Architecture and Urbanism, 1890–1915* (New York: Rizzoli, 1983).
6. Cass Gilbert to Clarence Johnston, June 22, 1879, Clarence Howard Johnston Papers, 1878–98, MHS.
7. Cass Gilbert had explored the possibility of becoming Daniel Burnham's partner after John Root's death in 1891, but neither man seemed willing to go beyond initial negotiations. See the letters in Box 17, File 2, Cass Gilbert Papers, MHS, among William Rutherford Mead, Cass Gilbert, Frank Stickel, and Daniel Burnham. See also Cass Gilbert to Lyman Gage, October 26, 1899, Cass Gilbert Collection, New York Custom House Letterbook, N-YHS.
8. The granddaughter of General Lewis Cass (1782–1866) had married into the Gilbert family. Lewis Cass himself had spent his early legal career in Zanesville as prosecuting attorney for Muskingum County. Cf. Robert Allen Jones, "Cass Gilbert: Midwestern Architect in New

York" (Ph.D. diss., Case Western Reserve University, Cleveland, 1976), 7.

9. Gilbert's paternal grandfather, Charles Champion Gilbert, had moved from Connecticut to Zanesville and shortly thereafter became Zanesville's first mayor.

10. Interview with Cass Gilbert by DeWitt McClellan Lockman, 1927, Lockman Manuscript, 1–2. Courtesy N-YHS.

11. The preparatory school, Winslow House, became Macalaster College, now in St. Paul. Gilbert met his future partner, James Knox Taylor, at the school. Marion D. Shutter and J. S. McLain, "Cass Gilbert," *Progressive Men of Minnesota* (Minneapolis: Minneapolis Journal, 1896), 134. There is very little information on Radcliffe (sometimes spelled Radcliff); David Gebhard and Tom Martinson in *A Guide to the Architecture of Minnesota* (Minneapolis: University of Minnesota Press, 1977), 282, illustrated only one building by him, the Dakota County Courthouse in Hastings (1869–70). He had set up a practice when Minnesota was still a territory and established an office in St. Paul in 1858. See Paul Clifford Larson, *Minnesota Architect: The Life and Work of Clarence Howard Johnston* (Afton, Minn.: Afton Historical Society Press, 1996), 5; and Ernest R. Sandeen, *St. Paul's Historic Summit Avenue* (St. Paul: Macalaster, 1978).

12. In 1878 there were only four places to study architecture formally in America: the Illinois Industrial University, Cornell University, Syracuse University, and M.I.T. The Illinois Industrial University (now the University of Illinois at Urbana-Champaign) had a separate architecture school after 1867, and, by 1873, architect Nathan Ricker was in charge of the courses. Cornell and Syracuse offered architectural programs beginning in 1871 and 1873, respectively. Michigan had opened a school in 1876 but it closed after only two years.

13. James Knox Taylor apparently stayed for two years; it is not clear if he received a diploma. Cf. James Knox Taylor to Jeremiah O'Rourke, Supervising Architect, September 5, 1893, Treasury Department Personnel Records, Record Group 56, NARA. Thanks go to Antoinette Lee and Joan Draper for showing me this letter. Clarence Johnston, whose family had moved to St. Paul in about 1864, worked in Radcliffe's office for three years prior to 1878, and only stayed at M.I.T. for a few months. Upon leaving Cambridge, he returned to Minnesota to work for E. P. Bassford in 1880. He then joined the firm of Herter Brothers in New York where he worked from 1881 to 1883. Patti Hoversten, "Clarence Howard Johnston, Sr.: An Introductory Biography" (Waseca, Minn., 1980), and Larson, *Minnesota Architect*.

14. Létang taught advanced design at M.I.T. until his death in 1890. See Shillaber, *Massachusetts Institute of Technology*.

15. Cass Gilbert to F. S. Swales, September 24, 1909, Box 8 (1909 file), Cass Gilbert Collection, Manuscript Division, LofC.

16. The Avery Architectural and Fine Arts Library has a sketch by Cass Gilbert of a Pompeiian room in their Rare Book Room, Columbia University, New York City. On Gilbert, Taylor, and Johnston at M.I.T., see Larson, *Minnesota Architect*.

17. Gilbert wrote letters home to his mother and to Clarence Johnston. These letters are on deposit in the Manuscript Division of the Library of Congress and also are quoted extensively by Robert Allen Jones in "Cass Gilbert: Midwestern Architect." He told of the money from his relatives; Cass Gilbert to Clarence Johnston, June 22, 1879, Clarence Howard Johnston Papers 1878–98, MHS. To his mother he wrote that he had received permission to copy drawings by Viollet-le-Duc on exhibit at the Hôtel de Cluny; Cass Gilbert to Elizabeth Wheeler Gilbert, May 23, 1880, File 1880, Box 2, Cass Gilbert Collection, Manuscript Division, LofC. One of Gilbert's watercolor copies after Viollet-le-Duc showing a portal from the church at Nervi is in the collection of the National Museum of American Art in Washington, D.C.

18. In a letter to Clarence Johnston, Gilbert's boyhood friend and later the state architect of Minnesota, Gilbert wrote: "Mr. [William] Ware . . . is now corresponding with Englishmen in my behalf, has forwarded a letter of mine to a friend in London who is to aid me in getting the coveted place in the office of either Street, Waterhouse, Burges, Shaw, or Siddon [*sic*]." See Cass Gilbert to Clarence Johnston, June 22, 1879, Clarence Johnston Papers, MHS.

19. Richard Guy Wilson, *McKim, Mead and White, Architects* (New York: Rizzoli, 1983), 15–16, 85. For more on the firm, see Paul R. Baker, *Stanny: The Gilded Life of Stanford White* (New York: Free Press, 1989), and Leland M. Roth, *McKim, Mead and White, Architects* (New York: Harper and Row, 1983).

20. Cass Gilbert to Cass Gilbert Jr., August 12, 1924, Personal Letters, Cass Gilbert Collection, Manuscript Division, LofC.

21. Cass Gilbert to Clarence Howard Johnston, August 24, 1882, Clarence Johnston Papers, MHS.

22. Gilbert detailed and supervised the construction of the Northern Pacific Beneficial Association Hospital (1882–83) in Brainerd, Minnesota, for McKim, Mead and White, one of the few Villard projects that was executed. Roth, *McKim, Mead and White, Architects*, 92. Villard was forced to resign from the Northern Pacific early in 1884 due to the company's financial state. And yet, Villard was involved with the company again by 1888 and remained on the board of directors until 1893, when the company went into receivership.

CHAPTER 1

1. I had always thought that Gilbert and Taylor joined forces in 1884; Paul Clifford Larson, in *Minnesota Architect: The Life and Work of Clarence Howard Johnston* (Afton, Minn.: Afton Historical Society Press, 1996), 41–42, demonstrates, however, that Taylor was working independently and/or collaborating with other architects prior to late 1885.

2. St. Paul's population rose rapidly between 1880 and 1895, growing from 40,000 to 140,292. Three thousand buildings valued at nine million dollars were erected in 1882 in St. Paul alone. Growth, however, was somewhat uneven given the pattern of boom and depression in the 1890s. Cf. M. L. Hartsough, *The Twin Cities as a Metropolitan Market,* Research Publications of the University of Minnesota Studies in the Social Sciences (Minneapolis: University of Minnesota, 1925), and Donald R. Torbert, "Minneapolis Architecture and Architects 1848–1908" (Ph.D. diss., University of Minnesota, Minneapolis, 1951),156–95.

3. William Towner Morgan, "The Politics of Business in the Career of an American Architect: Cass Gilbert, 1878–1905" (Ph.D. diss., University of Minnesota, Minneapolis, 1972), 46–47, quoting Cass Gilbert to Edward Spiers, February 28, 1885, Letterbook, Cass Gilbert Collection, N-YHS. Taylor had trained at M.I.T. (1877–79) and had worked as a draftsman in the New York offices of Charles Coolidge Haight and Bruce Price in the early 1880s. Taylor returned to St. Paul in 1882.

4. Taylor claimed he moved to Philadelphia because of his wife's health. There he went into partnership with Amos J. Boyden. The firm of Boyden and Taylor did not flourish in the depression of 1893. See James Knox Taylor to Jeremiah O'Rourke, September 5, 1893, and September 27, 1893, Treasury Department Personnel Records, Record Group 56, NARA. Antoinette Lee and Joan Draper shared these letters with me. In 1895 Taylor took a drafting job in the Office of the Supervising Architect in Washington, D.C., where he eventually was promoted to supervising architect in 1898. Following his tenure as supervising architect (1898–1912), he opened an office in Boston and then moved to Yonkers, New York. He died in Tampa, Florida, about 1929.

5. John Wellborn Root, "The City House in the West," in *The Meanings of Architecture: Buildings and Writings by John Wellborn Root,* ed. Donald Hoffmann (New York: Horizon Press, 1967), 232.

6. For more on Taylor's father and Taylor's work with Clarence Howard Johnston, see Larson, *Minnesota Architect,* 33.

7. After the death of Gilbert's father, the Gilbert estate, consisting of the mother, Elizabeth W. Gilbert, and her three sons, Charles, Cass, and Samuel, apparently was formed to handle the family's real-estate interests. Gilbert's mother died on January 16, 1897, and the managing agent, Stiles W. Burr, summarized the investments for one of the Gilbert creditors. At Elizabeth's death, the family owned at least six properties in St. Paul. Burr to Messrs. Markham, Moore, and Markham, November 11, 1898, Box 18, Cass Gilbert Papers, MHS.

8. See H. M. Finch's obituary in an unlabeled notebook, Box 26, Cass Gilbert Collection, Manuscript Division, LofC. Julia Gilbert's mother, Emily S. Finch, died in Milwaukee on June 5, 1903. Cf. Box 20, 1903, Cass Gilbert Papers, MHS. See also "Mrs. Cass Gilbert Led in Philanthropy," *New York Times,* September 5, 1952, 27.

Cass and Julia Gilbert had four children: Emily, Elizabeth (d. 1904), Julia, and Cass Jr. To my knowledge, Emily never married, Julia married Charles Post and had four children, and Cass Jr. married a woman named Jarvis with whom he had five children.

9. The president of the Minnesota Club was Henry H. Sibley. George Squires, Gilbert's attorney, was also involved. Gilbert was the only architect among the founding members. Cf. Minnesota Club, *The Organization and Government of the Minnesota Club* (St. Paul, 1886), and Patricia Murphy, "Minnesota's Architectural Favorite Son," *AIA Journal,* March 1981, 76. When the Minnesota Club needed to expand, they turned to Gilbert in 1892 and again in 1899 for additions to their (now demolished) building.

10. Robert Bruegmann, in *The Architects and the City: Holabird and Roche of Chicago, 1880–1918* (Chicago: University of Chicago Press, 1997), 255ff., gives an excellent account of the rise of golf clubs in America after 1880.

11. A small group of architects, initially on the East Coast, had been attempting to establish themselves as experts for over twenty-five years. In Minnesota, despite rivalries among themselves and with out-of-state firms, architects united to form the Minnesota Chapter of the American Institute of Architects in 1892. See Steven Buetow, "The Founding Fathers," *Architecture Minnesota* 18 (November/December 1992): 32–53, and Henry H. Saylor, *The AIA's First Hundred Years* (Washington, D.C.: The Octagon, 1957).

12. Record of Work December 1891 to June 1902, 56–58, Cass Gilbert Collection, N-YHS; and letter to author from Elisabeth Doermann, administrator, James J. Hill House, January 24, 1983.

13. An example of an in-house designer is James Brodie (1843–1935), an architect and engineer for the Great Northern Railway. Many of the structures built for James J. Hill were designed by Brodie. The Minnesota Historical Society has a copy of his diary. My thanks to Irene Brodie for showing me the original.

14. For Gilbert's early career, see Patricia Murphy, "The Early Career of Cass Gilbert: 1878–1895," (master's thesis, University of Virginia, Charlottesville, 1979). This useful work was followed by an exhibit, organized by Murphy in 1984, accompanied by the pamphlet *Cass Gilbert, Master Architect* (Minneapolis: University of Minnesota Gallery).

15. See Vincent J. Scully Jr., *The Shingle Style and the Stick Style: Architectural Theory and Design from Downing to the Origins of Wright* (New Haven: Yale University Press [1955], 1971).

16. See Wheaton Holden, "The Peabody Touch: Peabody and Stearns of Boston, 1870–1917," *Journal of the Society of Architectural Historians* 32 (May 1973): 125–27, and Sarah Bradford Landau, "The Tall Office Building Artistically Reconsidered: Arcaded Buildings of the New York School, c.1870–1890," in *In Search of Modern Architecture: A Tribute to Henry Russell Hitchcock,* ed. Helen Searing (New York: Architectural History Foundation; Cambridge: M.I.T. Press, 1982), 136–64.

17. Thomas Tallmadge, *The Story of England's Architecture* (New York: W. W. Norton, 1934). For explorations of eclecticism in architecture, see Richard Longstreth, "Academic Eclecticism in American Architecture," *Winterthur Portfolio* 17 (spring 1982): 55–82, and Carroll L. V. Meeks, "Picturesque Eclecticism," *Art Bulletin* 32 (1950): 226–35.

18. See Bainbridge Bunting, *Houses of Boston's Back Bay: An Architectural History, 1840–1917* (Cambridge, Mass.: Belknap Press, 1967).

19. The proportions of Gilbert's Kent Street entry are different from those used by Henry Hobson Richardson, but pushing the stairs back under a broad arch was an arrangement Richardson employed at the Trinity Church Rectory (1879) in Boston and in his Hay house (1884–86) in Washington, D.C. Standard works on Richardson include Margaret Henderson Floyd, *Henry Hobson Richardson: A Genius for Architecture* (New York: The Monacelli Press, 1997); Henry-Russell Hitchcock, *The Architecture of H. H. Richardson and His Times* (Cambridge, Mass.: M.I.T. Press, 1966); Jeffrey Karl Ochsner, *H. H. Richardson: Complete Architectural Works* (Cambridge, Mass.: M.I.T. Press [1982], 1984); O'Gorman, *Henry Hobson Richardson and His Office: Selected Drawings* (Cambridge, Mass.: Harvard College Library, 1974); O'Gorman, *H. H. Richardson: Architectural Forms for an American Society* (Chicago: University of Chicago Press, 1987); and James F. O'Gorman, *Living Architecture: A Biography of Henry Hobson Richardson* (New York: Simon and Schuster, 1997).

20. Undated scrapbooks in the Cass Gilbert Collection, N-YHS, contain clippings of building details, plans, interiors, and graphics. Relevant to the Bookstaver Row Houses are details from Richardson's Trinity Church Rectory, showing stairs tucked under the arch. Thanks to Mary Beth Betts for unearthing these scrapbooks.

21. Paul Clifford Larson, "H. H. Richardson Goes West: The Rise and Fall of an Eastern Star," in *The Spirit of H. H. Richardson on the Midland Prairies,* ed. Paul Clifford Larson with Susan M. Brown (Minneapolis: University Art Museum, 1988), 29.

22. Murphy, "Early Career of Cass Gilbert," 79.

23. On W. R. Emerson, see Cynthia Zaitzevsky, *The Architecture of William Ralph Emerson, 1833–1917* (exh. cat., Cambridge, Mass.: Harvard University. Fogg Art Museum, 1969). In letters written home, Gilbert would describe buildings that caught his eye. One instance was a house by Emerson that Gilbert described to Clarence Johnston. See Gilbert to Johnston, June 22, 1879, Clarence Howard Johnston Papers, MHS.

24. Murphy, "Early Career of Cass Gilbert," 73.

25. Patricia Murphy's thesis is an excellent source on Gilbert and Taylor's church designs. See "Early Career of Cass Gilbert," chapter 3.

26. Montgomery Schuyler, "Glimpses of Western Architecture: St. Paul and Minneapolis," *Harper's* 83 (October 1891): 736–55, reprinted in Schuyler, *American Architecture and Other Writings,* ed. William H. Jordy and Ralph Coe (Cambridge, Mass.: Harvard University Press, 1967), I:303. The editors and Schuyler also noted that Gilbert's Dayton Avenue Presbyterian Church was modeled on Richardson's Church of the Unity (1866–69) in Springfield, Massachusetts.

Cass Gilbert added a chapel and Sunday school spaces to the original plan (1902, 1909–10, 1911).

27. Emmanuel Swedenborg, born in 1688, was a Swede who moved to England toward the end of his life. His teachings began to be known in the United States around 1790. Among architects, Daniel Burnham was known for his Swedenborgian background, and his partner, John Root, was also a practitioner. See Thomas S. Hines, *Burnham of Chicago: Architect and Planner* (Chicago: University of Chicago Press, 1974).

28. *The Virginia Street Church (Swedenborgian)* (St. Paul: The Church, 1979), unpaginated. This flier is held in MHS. The St. Paul congregation was first organized in 1860 and reactivated in 1873.

29. For more on this church, see James Taylor Dunn's pamphlet *Cass Gilbert and the German Presbyterian Bethlehem Church* (St. Paul: Minnesota Historical Society, 1968). I am grateful to Mr. Dunn for sending a copy to me.

30. Sketchbook, File 15, Cass Gilbert Collection, NMAH. The back page contains a drawing made in Belgium of the German Bethlehem Presbyterian Church with a note dated September 9, 1922: "A memory of the little church at the foot of the hill, St. Paul."

31. The lych gate was rebuilt in 1987 by parishioner Neil Hiedeman with mortise and tenon joinery. A lych gate originally served as the place where pallbearers would meet the rector before proceeding into the church with the coffin.

32. Cass Gilbert to Clarence Johnston, August 3, 1879, Clarence Johnston Papers, MHS.

33. Gilbert was awarded this commission by Bishop Mahlon Gilbert (no relation), who had also been involved with the Camp Memorial Chapel (1888) that Gilbert and Taylor designed on Lake Minnetonka in Minneapolis. See Murphy, "Early Career of Cass Gilbert," 59–60.

34. Thanks to Marion Matters of St. Paul for information about St. Clement's Episcopal Church. The church office has a flier containing information about the church's history. See also "St. Clement's Memorial Church, St. Paul, Minnesota," *American Architect and Building News* 48 (June 8, 1895): 103.

35. Gilbert exclaimed to his son, "The small house business—no!" in 1932. Cass Gilbert to Cass Gilbert Jr., July 8, 1932, Personal Letters, Cass Gilbert Collection, N-YHS. On Gilbert's Minnesota depots, see Paul Clifford Larson, "Lost Minnesota [Willmar Railroad Park]," *Architecture Minnesota* 14 (July/August 1988): 66, and Marvin Welinski and William F. Rapp, "Little Falls, Minnesota—A Cass Gilbert Design," *Bulletin of the Railroad Station Historical Society* 19 (July/August 1986): 60. The Willmar station has been demolished, and the Anoka depot is much altered.

36. The firm's first commercial project was built in 1885: the Duluth Board of Trade (destroyed by fire in 1893).

37. The most likely connection to bring Gilbert and Taylor the Endicott Building was Luther Stearns Cushing. For more on Cushing, see Chapter 2.

38. Mary C. Crawford, *Famous Families of Massachusetts* (Boston: Little Brown and Co., 1930), I:77.

39. See, for example, William Endicott to Cass Gilbert, November 20, 1901; Henry Endicott to Cass Gilbert, June 22, 1894; and "Norris Estate

Building," July 3, 1894, all in Cass Gilbert Papers, MHS.

40. For further details on this commission, see Sharon Irish, "West Hails East: Cass Gilbert in Minnesota," *Minnesota History* 53, no. 5 (spring 1993): 196–207.

41. The renovation of the Endicott Building in 1981 included a curved ceiling with simplified colored glass in the arcade. The fragile drawings for the Endicott Building are held in the Northwest Architectural Archives, St. Paul, Minnesota.

42. The structural engineer was Louis Ritter, of Chicago, who designed the building's interior framing and foundations, and made it possible to build next door to a newspaper plant without disturbing the presses.

43. Francis S. Swales, "Mr. Cass Gilbert of New York and St. Paul," *Builder*, January 12, 1912, 32, annotated copy in Miscellany, Cass Gilbert Collection, Manuscript Division, LofC.

44. To Clarence Johnston, Gilbert wrote: "The Villard house is up to the 2nd floor beams and has a good character. It is amusing to see how jealous Wells is of his masterpiece." Cass Gilbert to Clarence Johnston, September 10, 1882, Clarence Johnston Papers, MHS.

45. Wells had written to Gilbert in 1884 about this project. Joseph Morrill Wells to Cass Gilbert, July 30, 1884, General Correspondence, Cass Gilbert Collection, Manuscript Division, LofC. Leland Roth states that the RussWin Hotel was in turn based on McKim, Mead and White's Benedict Apartments. See Leland M. Roth, *McKim, Mead and White, Architects* (New York: Harper and Row, 1983), 94.

46. Joseph Morrill Wells to Cass Gilbert, November 6, 1889, General Correspondence, Cass Gilbert Collection, Manuscript Division, LofC.

47. For information on the Minnesota State Capitol competition, see Irish, "West Hails East," 204.

48. Cass Gilbert to Frederick C. Gibbs, February 4, 1898, Cass Gilbert Papers, MHS.

49. Lyman Farwell (former McKim, Mead and White employee) to Cass Gilbert, November 12, 1894, Minnesota Capitol Correspondence, Cass Gilbert Papers, MHS.

50. Gilbert acknowledged his debt to McKim, Mead and White in another annotation on the Swales article. See Miscellany, Cass Gilbert Collection, Manuscript Division, LofC. There was a delay in starting construction of the Rhode Island Capitol, so both were being built at the same time: 1895–1905.

51. Gunvald Aus (1861?–1950), who worked with Gilbert regularly after 1900, designed the structural system for the capitol dome. On the mechanical and heating systems for the capitol, see "The Mechanical Plant of the Minnesota State Capitol," *Engineering Record* 49 (April 16, 1904): 474–78, and "Heating and Ventilating the Minnesota State Capitol," *Engineering Record* 49 (May 21, 1904): 652–55. These systems were designed by the M.I.T.-trained engineer Burt Sylvanus Harrison (1870–?), who had worked with Gilbert since 1899.

52. See *The American Renaissance 1876–1917, Guide to the Exhibition and Illustrated Catalogue* (New York: Brooklyn Museum, 1979), especially the sections by Richard Guy Wilson, and Michael Conforti, ed., *Minnesota 1900: Art and Life on the Upper Mississippi, 1890–1915* (Newark, Del.: University of Delaware Press, 1994).

53. For a wonderful narrative and good color photographs of the capitol interior, see Thomas O'Sullivan, *North Star Statehouse: An Armchair Guide to the Minnesota State Capitol* (St. Paul, Minn.: Pogo Press, 1994).

54. In 1903 workers began finishing the interior decoration and the exterior terracing; the government staff moved into their new quarters in 1905. The entire job was completed in 1907. For years after the completion of the capitol, Cass Gilbert hoped to execute his plan for the capitol approaches. While this never came to pass, there is a good deal of literature on the proposals, including Scott Lyle Koch, "Cass Gilbert's Minnesota Capitol Approach Plan, 1902–1915" (master's thesis, Illinois State University, Bloomington, 1975); Charles Mulford Robinson, "Ambitions of Three Cities," *Architectural Record* 21 (May 1907): 337–46; *Plan of St. Paul* (1932); and *Report of Capitol Approaches Commission to the Common Council of the City of St. Paul* (1907). The last two items are in the collection of the Minnesota Historical Society.

55. Cass Gilbert to James Knox Taylor, January 4, 1898 (actually 1899), Broadway Chambers Letterbook, Cass Gilbert Collection, N-YHS.

56. December 5, 1889, Personal Letterbook, Cass Gilbert Collection, N-YHS, on Holyoke's employment; Thomas Holyoke to Cass Gilbert, November 14, 1890, February 15, 1891, and March 23, 1891, Cass Gilbert Papers, MHS, on Holyoke's travels in Europe. See also "Thomas Holyoke Dead," *St. Paul Pioneer Press*, March 30, 1925, 14; *St. Paul Dispatch*, March 30, 1925, 5.

57. Professor Pierre-Richard Bisson of the University of Montréal confirmed Haskell's death date for me, citing "Mort de M S. Haskell," *Le Devoir* (Montreal), May 21, 1913, 8. For correspondence between Haskell and Gilbert, see April 29, 1891, and July 5, 1891, Box 17, File 2; February 23, 1899, Box 18, Cass Gilbert Papers, MHS; March 6, 1899, Broadway Chambers Letterbook; October 9, 1903, Miscellaneous Correspondence; and Journal, January 8, 1904, 26, Cass Gilbert Collection, N-YHS.

58. See "John Rockart Dies; Noted Architect," *New York Times*, October 14, 1951, 88.

59. Cass Gilbert to F. S. Swales, September 24, 1909, Box 8 (1909 file), Cass Gilbert Collection, Manuscript Division, LofC.

Chapter 2

1. Edwin M. Bacon, *The Book of Boston: 50 Years' Recollections of the New England Metropolis* (Boston: Book of Boston Co., 1916). In 1886 Porter organized the Boston Real Estate Trust with two million dollars in subscriptions. Richard Herndon, *Boston of Today; a Glance at Its History and Characteristics* (Boston: Post Publishing Co., 1892), 352–53; Henrietta M. Larson, *Guide to Business History: Materials for the Study of American Business and Suggestions for Their Use* (Cambridge: Harvard University Press, 1948).

2. Cushing's concern had offices in Chicago, Omaha, Denver, and Kansas City, as well as in St. Paul. Cushing, who had arrived in St. Paul in 1886, was the son of a prominent Massachusetts judge and kept up his Boston ties. See his "Obituary," from

June 23, 1856, in the Luther S. Cushing Papers, MHS, as well as "L. S. Cushing, Realtor, Dies," *St. Paul Pioneer Press,* October 12, 1937, 1.

3. The Brazer Building Trust, also known as the Norris Estate Building, was a real-estate investment group consisting of the Norris family of Milwaukee, attorneys Thomas and Arthur Russell, and the banker Moses Williams. See Henry Endicott to Cass Gilbert, June 22, 1894, and "Norris Estate Building," July 3, 1894, both in Cass Gilbert Papers, MHS. The Brazer Building, only a few doors away from the Boston Stock Exchange, had mainly financial tenants. Boston Landmarks Commission, "Second Brazer Building," June 1980. Thanks to Gail Fenske for sending me this information.

4. Cf. William Kilham, *Boston after Bulfinch* (Cambridge, Mass.: Harvard University Press, 1946), and "Brazer Building, Boston, Massachusetts," *American Architect and Building News* 56 (May 22, 1897): 64.

5. Kenneth Boulding, *The Organizational Revolution* (New York: Harper, 1961). See also Alfred D. Chandler, *The Visible Hand: The Managerial Revolution in American Business* (Cambridge: Harvard University Press, 1977), and Alan Trachtenberg, *The Incorporation of America: Culture and Society in the Gilded Age* (New York: Hill and Wang, 1982).

6. See Carol Willis, *Form Follows Finance: Skyscrapers and Skylines in New York and Chicago* (New York: Princeton Architectural Press, 1995). Her book offers a good bibliography on this topic.

7. Edward Andrews's paternal grandfather, Ebenezer Turrell Andrews, had left a large fortune that allowed the next two generations (at least) to explore their interests at leisure. Edward Andrews attended Harvard, receiving an A.B. in 1853 and an A.M. in 1857. Between degrees he toured Europe and met the woman who became his wife in 1855, Sarah Hannah Addoms. In the forty odd years that intervened between Andrews's marriage and the construction of the Broadway Chambers Building, built for Sarah Addoms Andrews's estate, Edward Andrews pursued agricultural interests in New England, dabbled in business in Boston, worked as a banker in Paris, and researched innovations in transportation and communications. Edward Andrews, "Letter to Samuel S. Shaw," *Report of the Harvard Class of 1853* (Cambridge, 1913), 25–30; Richard Herndon, *Men of Progress: 1000 Biographical Sketches and Portraits of Leaders in Business and Professional Life in Massachusetts* (Boston: New England Magazine, 1896). See also Jeffrey Karl Ochsner, "H. H. Richardson's Frank William Andrews House," *Journal of the Society of Architectural Historians* 43 (1984): 20–32. Frank was Edward's older brother.

8. As a young man, Harry Black had worked for a surveying party in the Pacific Northwest, sold woolen goods in the West for a Chicago firm, and started a bank in Washington State. Upon his arrival in Chicago, he married George Fuller's daughter after a brief courtship. Upon Fuller's death in 1900, Black took charge of his father-in-law's firm.

9. Cass Gilbert to Alexander Porter, February 8, 1899, Broadway Chambers Letterbook, Cass Gilbert Collection, N-YHS.

10. [Cass Gilbert], "The Financial Importance of Rapid Building," *Engineering Record* 41 (June 30, 1900): 624.

11. Memo specifications of Brazer Building, Box 2, Cass Gilbert Papers, MHS.

12. Cass Gilbert to F. W. Chandler, June 14, 1897, Box 2, Cass Gilbert Papers, MHS.

13. Andrews wrote to Gilbert on April 18, 1899: "I should much regret to give up and return to the idea of terra cotta both on account of the increased expense and because we should lose the strong characteristics which the brick we had decided upon would give us and contrast with almost all the other high buildings which are either stone or terra cotta." See also Edward Andrews to Cass Gilbert, April 25, 1899, Box 18, Cass Gilbert Papers, MHS.

14. See Sarah Bradford Landau, "The Tall Office Building Artistically Reconsidered: Arcaded Buildings of the New York School, c.1870–1890," in *In Search of Modern Architecture: A Tribute to Henry Russell Hitchcock,* ed. Helen Searing (New York: Architectural History Foundation; Cambridge: M.I.T. Press, 1982), and Landau and Carl W. Condit, *Rise of the New York Skyscraper, 1865–1913* (New Haven: Yale University Press, 1996).

15. In the Daily Memo, February 20, 1899, to March 3, 1899, Box 3, Cass Gilbert Papers, MHS, Gilbert recounted: "I met Mr. William Andrews at the hotel . . . [W]e went up to Columbia College and looked over the buildings, and I showed him the Harvard brick used there. We were together until late in the afternoon, having looked over a number of buildings in the meanwhile, particularly the St. James Building."

16. Edward Andrews to Cass Gilbert, February 2, 1899, Box 18, Cass Gilbert Papers, MHS.

17. Both William Bonner and a Fuller promotional brochure stated that the Fuller Company opened a New York office in 1896. They waited two and one-half years for the Broadway Chambers project to materialize. See Bonner, *New York: The New Metropolis, 1623–1923* (New York, 1924), 992, and *Broadway Chambers: A Modern Office Building* (New York, 1900), 12. Raymond Daly claimed that Clinton and Russell's Broad Street Exchange was Fuller's first contract in New York, but Sarah Bradford Landau checked the building records and established for me that the Broadway Chambers was begun and completed before the Broad Street Exchange. Correspondence from Landau to author, March 13, 1984; Daly, "Seventy-Five Years of Construction Pioneering: George A. Fuller Company, 1882–1957," *Newcomen Society in North America* 24 (1957): unpaginated.

18. Cass Gilbert to Edward Andrews, February 8, 1899, Broadway Chambers Letterbook, Cass Gilbert Collection, N-YHS.

19. Robert Bruegmann, in *The Architects and the City: Holabird and Roche of Chicago, 1880–1918* (Chicago: University of Chicago Press, 1997), 81, notes that the Tacoma Building in Chicago (1888), built by the George A. Fuller Company, "was perhaps the earliest large-scale demonstration of the use of the single-contract general contractor, a business practice that revolutionized large-scale construction throughout the country."

20. With the aim of becoming one of the largest contractors in the country, the Fuller Company had

refined its organization in Chicago in the 1880s. The company charted the multiple phases of construction and assigned specific employees to each task. For more on Fuller's organizational innovations, see Webb Waldron and Paul Starrett, *Changing the Skyline* (New York: Whittlesey House, McGraw Hill, 1939), and Daly, "Seventy-Five Years of Construction Pioneering." On Fuller's activities in Chicago, consult Bruegmann, *Architects and the City*, and David Van Zanten, "The Nineteenth Century: The Projecting of Chicago as a Commercial City and the Rationalization of Design and Construction," in *Chicago and New York: Architectural Interactions*, ed. John Zukowsky (Chicago: Art Institute of Chicago, 1984).

21. Black, Gilbert, and Luther Cushing, a real-estate agent in Minnesota, helped arrange a loan for Andrews through the Scottish Provident Institute of Edinburgh. Luther Cushing to Cass Gilbert, February 27, 1896, Box 2, Cass Gilbert Papers, MHS. The four representatives for the Scottish loan company were Owen Aldis, Arthur T. Aldis, Northcote, and Watson. The Aldises were among the largest real-estate managers and loan agents in the country, with offices in Chicago and extensive connections in England. For more on the Aldises, see Robert Bruegmann, *Holabird and Roche/Holabird and Root* (New York: Garland, 1991), I:120, 160, and Bruegmann, *Architects and the City*, passim.

22. H. S. Black to Cass Gilbert, November 12, 1896, Box 3, Cass Gilbert Papers, MHS.

23. Daily Memo, February 20, 1899, to March 3, 1899, Box 3, Cass Gilbert Papers, MHS.

24. After a brief tenure with Fuller, Theodore Starrett quit and joined Henry S. Thompson to form the Thompson-Starrett Company, which became Fuller's greatest rival. For more on Starrett and his brothers, see Waldron and Starrett, *Changing the Skyline*, and Louis J. Horowitz, *The Towers of New York: Memoirs of a Master Builder* (New York: Simon and Schuster, 1937).

25. The Broadway Chambers site was clear sand to a depth of at least fifty feet. A grillage foundation of steel beams embedded in concrete rested on the sand. Due to the proximity of neighboring buildings, combined footings supported the wall columns from within the grillage. The adjacent buildings were shored up by needles resting on heavy timbers while new foundation walls with concrete footings were built under them.

26. [Gilbert], "Financial Importance of Rapid Building," 624.

27. Daily Memo, March 3, 1899, Box 3, Cass Gilbert Papers, MHS. Harry Black had recommended Purdy and Henderson to Gilbert as the engineers for the Astoria Hotel (Henry Hardenbergh, 1895–97) and the St. Paul Building, New York (George Browne Post, 1895–98). Corydon Purdy (1859?–1944) had graduated as a civil engineer from the University of Wisconsin in 1885 and, after working in Chicago, had opened a New York office in 1894. With Henderson, he specialized in tall buildings and subway construction.

28. Reginald Pelham Bolton, "The Equipment of Tall Office Buildings in New York City," *Engineering Record* 39 (May 13, 1899): 551.

29. Theodore Starrett, *Skyscraper Building: Being Essays on Modern Building Construction and the Tendencies Thereof in Our Great Cities* (New York, 1907), 13.

30. Susan Tunick in *Terra-Cotta Skyline: New York's Architectural Ornament* (New York: Princeton Architectural Press, 1997), 55, claims that the Broadway Chambers has "the earliest surviving polychrome terra cotta in New York." The glazes on the terra cotta were by the Perth Amboy Terra Cotta Company. See also "Polychromatic Terra Cotta Effects on the Broadway-Chambers, New York," *Brick* 13 (August 1900): 91.

31. Samuel-Stevens Haskell to Cass Gilbert, June 22, 1899, Box 3, Cass Gilbert Papers, MHS.

32. [Gilbert], "Financial Importance of Rapid Building," 624.

33. William Robert Ware, "An Unaffected School of Modern Architecture in America—Will It Come?," *Catalog of the T-Square Club Exhibition and Architectural Annual* (1898), 23.

34. Cass Gilbert to Julia Finch Gilbert, September 24, 1899, Box 6, 1899, Cass Gilbert Collection, Manuscript Division, LofC.

35. Cass Gilbert to Julia Finch Gilbert, April 8, 1900, Box 6, 1900, Cass Gilbert Collection, Manuscript Division, LofC; Cass Gilbert to Post and Reese Realtors, August 15, 1902, Box 19, Cass Gilbert Papers, MHS.

36. See Landau and Condit, *Rise of the New York Skyscraper*, 111–13.

37. I have found William R. Taylor's *In Pursuit of Gotham: Culture and Commerce in New York* (New York: Oxford University Press, 1992) to be very helpful in thinking about civic embellishment.

38. See William Towner Morgan, "The Politics of Business in the Career of an American Architect: Cass Gilbert, 1878–1905" (Ph.D. diss., University of Minnesota, Minneapolis, 1972), and Sharon Irish, "Cass Gilbert's New York Custom House, Bowling Green" (master's thesis, Northwestern University, Evanston, Ill., 1982), and Irish, "Cass Gilbert's New York Career, 1899–1905" (Ph.D. diss., Northwestern University, Evanston, Ill., 1985). A thorough Historic Structure Report on the Custom House, written by Bonnie Marxer and Heli Meltsner, was prepared by the Society for the Preservation of New England Antiquities (Boston) in 1982.

39. Bruegmann, in *Architects and the City*, 347, discusses how the Custom House design served as a model for many other public and private monumental buildings in the early twentieth century.

40. Gilbert collected references and sent his brother, Samuel, and Samuel-Stevens Haskell to Washington, D.C., to represent his interests. The daily office memos dated April 26 to May 4, 1899, are the most useful for this story. They are with the Cass Gilbert Papers, MHS.

41. "The Custom House Plans," *New York Times*, October 25, 1899, 7.

42. Sharon Irish, "Beaux-Arts Teamwork in an American Architectural Office: Cass Gilbert's Entry to the New York Custom House Competition," *New Mexico Studies in the Fine Arts* 7 (1982): 10–13; on Hébrard specifically, see Louis Hautecoeur, "Ernest M. Hébrard," *Urbanisme* (1933): 141–43, and Pierre Lavedan, "Ernest Hébrard," *L'Architecture* 46 (April 15, 1933): 109–12.

43. Samuel-Stevens Haskell to Cass Gilbert, July 29, 1899, New York Custom House Letterbook, Cass Gilbert Collection, N-YHS.

44. Samuel-Stevens Haskell to Cass Gilbert, September 2, 1899, Box 19 (1899), Cass Gilbert Papers, MHS.

45. Supervising architect Taylor requested nominations for judges from the competitors in July 1899. Thomas R. Kimball from Omaha and Frank Miles Day of Philadelphia were chosen; Taylor himself completed the jury.

46. Cass Gilbert to George Squires, October 7, 1899, Box 6, 1899, file 1, Cass Gilbert Collection, Manuscript Division, LofC.

47. This letter reads, in part, "I enclose herein a study for the facade of the New York Custom House. While I do not consider this as absolutely final, it is . . . what I wish to place before the department . . . I want the detail to be rich, but have more of the Roman type than expressed in the original drawings, simpler and more severe." Cass Gilbert to Samuel-Stevens Haskell, January 3, 1900, New York Custom House Letterbook, Cass Gilbert Collection, N-YHS.

48. Johnson finished a watercolor perspective of the Custom House with a sloping roof on March 23, 1901 (not illustrated here).

49. William P. Foulds started in Gilbert's office in 1899 while he was a student at the Pratt Institute. In 1903 he left Gilbert's employ to study in Paris; he was admitted to the first class in 1905 and received financial assistance from Gilbert in that year and the next. Foulds sent Gilbert letters and drawings while he was abroad and returned to the office in 1908. Correspondence between the men is held at the Minnesota Historical Society and the Library of Congress in their Cass Gilbert Collections. For Foulds's later work, see his fluid charcoal sketches for a proposed St. Louis Art Museum expansion (1915) that never progressed past preliminary studies. These studies are held in the Cass Gilbert Collection at the N-YHS.

50. Thomas Robert Johnson was a Canadian from Toronto. Johnson went abroad briefly in 1903 and then returned to be involved in most of Gilbert's major projects up to 1915. Johnson's papers and drawings are held at the Avery Architectural and Fine Arts Library of Columbia University, and an assessment of his work was published by Alfred M. Githens, "Monographs on Architectural Renderers . . . of Today," Brickbuilder 23 (May 1914): 110–12.

51. I appreciate the 1997 conversation with Mary Beth Betts in which she underscored the orientation of the Custom House away from the waterfront.

52. There were numerous contemporary articles on the Custom House, including "Design for a Custom House," American Architect and Building News 67 (March 24, 1900): plates; "Design for a New York Custom House," Architectural Review 7 (1900): plates 21–26; Cass Gilbert, "The New York Custom House," Architects' and Builders' Magazine 9 (November 1907): 51–61; "Heating and Ventilating the New Custom House in New York," Engineering Record 53 (May 26, 1906): 649–53; "Northwest View of the U.S. Custom House, New York," American Architect and Building News 89 (March 31, 1906): 115 and plates; Montgomery Schuyler, "The New Custom House at New York," Architectural Record 8 (July 1906): 1–14; and "Some Structural Features of the New Custom House at New York," Engineering Record 53 (May 19, 1906): 628–30. See also Brendan Gill's monograph, The U.S. Custom House on Bowling Green (New York: New York Landmarks Conservancy, 1976).

53. For an overview of this widely adopted method of construction, see George R. Collins, "The Transfer of Thin Masonry Vaulting from Spain to America," Journal of the Society of Architectural Historians 27 (October 1968): 176–201; and Janet Parks and Alan G. Neumann, The Old World Builds the New: The Guastavino Company and the Technology of the Catalan Vault, 1885–1962 (New York: Columbia University in the City of New York, 1996).

54. "Some Structural Features," 628–30.

55. Cass Gilbert to James Knox Taylor, August 30 and November 29, 1901, Box 399, Record Group 121, WNRC; the August letter read, in part, "citizens of New York deem it [granite] absolutely necessary to the success of the building as a monument." Peirce held major interest in the Bodwell Granite Company, which supplied the pink and grey Fox Island granite. John Peirce to James Knox Taylor, November 29, 1901, Box 399, Record Group 121, WNRC.

56. A grillage foundation of concrete and steel rested on hardpan clay or boulder formations with a load of four tons per square foot.

57. Ada Louise Huxtable, "New Custom House: Modern, Functional, No Match for Old," New York Times, October 4, 1973, 47.

58. Cass Gilbert to James Knox Taylor, August 21, 1903, Box 401, Record Group 121, WNRC. Thomas Johnson also visited the quarries. See his report April 1, 1904, Box 401, Record Group 121, WNRC; Peirce defended himself: John Peirce to Cass Gilbert, July 2, 1904, Box 402, Record Group 121, WNRC.

59. John Peirce to H. A. Taylor, October 5, 1903, Box 401, Record Group 121, WNRC.

60. Cass Gilbert to John Peirce, April 18, 1903, Box 401, Record Group 121, WNRC.

61. Cass Gilbert to John Peirce, June 22, 1904, Box 402, Record Group 121, WNRC. An estimated five months was needed to carve the large granite capitals.

62. Cass Gilbert to James Knox Taylor, December 30, 1901, Box 399, Record Group 121, WNRC.

63. On D. C. French, see Kathryn Greenthal and Michael Richman, "Daniel Chester French's 'Continents,'" American Art Journal 8 (November 1976): 47–58, and Michael Richman, Daniel Chester French: An American Sculptor (Washington, D.C.: National Trust for Historic Preservation, 1976).

64. A Harvard graduate (1877), John DuFais had an office at 257 Fifth Avenue and was already a member of the Harvard Club, the Calumet Club, several patriotic societies, and the Baltusrol Golf Club. Cf. The Social Register, 1901.

65. The Union Club was razed after 1961.

66. Samuel-Stevens Haskell to Cass Gilbert, July 5, 1900, Box 19 (1900), Cass Gilbert Papers, MHS.

67. Wells was promoted to office chief when Haskell left in 1903. Aus worked with Gilbert as a consultant rather than as an employee, but kept his offices in the same building as Gilbert. See Kenneth Bjork, *Saga in Steel and Concrete: Norwegian Engineers in America* (Northfield, Minn.: Norwegian-American Historical Association, 1947), and "Gunvald Aus," *New York Times,* June 7, 1950, 29.

68. For more information on the courthouse and its decoration, see Leslie D. Ward and Cass Gilbert, *Essex County Court House* (Newark: Essex County Building Commission, 1908); Ernest A. Reed, *Essex County Court House and Hall of Records* (Newark, 1931); and Kenyon Cox to Cass Gilbert, September 29, 1907, Cass Gilbert Collection, N-YHS.

69. George B. Post; Babb, Cook and Willard; Carrère and Hastings; and McKim, Mead and White were the other competitors. The new structure was to replace the Egyptian Revival work (1837–38) of John Haviland at a cost of $750,000, although it eventually cost $1,948,000.

70. The American Insurance Company Building is no longer extant. Its bronze doors, by Andrew O'Connor, are now in the Newark Museum.

CHAPTER 3

1. For the Trans-Mississippi Exposition in 1898 in Omaha, he had designed the Agricultural Building. For Chicago, he had submitted a design for the Minnesota Building but lost to William Channing Whitney. Gilbert's designs for that exposition are in the New-York Historical Society.

2. The other members of the Commission of Architects were James Knox Taylor, John I. Haynes, Frank Howe, William Eames, Thomas C. Young, Theodore C. Link, Thomas Rogers Kimball, C. Howard Walker, Frederick Widman, Boisselier, John Carrère, and Thomas Hastings.

3. See Alan Lathrop, "Emmanuel L. Masqueray 1861–1917," *Minnesota History* 47 (summer 1980): 43–56.

4. C. Howard Walker is generally credited with the plan of the Louisiana Purchase Exposition. Louis LaBeaume, "Looking Backwards at St. Louis Architecture," *Missouri Historical Society Bulletin* 14 (January 1958): 186. For more information on the exposition, see "The Building of a World's Fair: How the Louisiana Purchase Exposition Has Been Constructed," *Engineering Record* 49 (May 7, 1904): 568–80; David R. Francis, *The Universal Exposition of 1904* (St. Louis: Louisiana Purchase Exposition, 1913); Montgomery Schuyler, "The Architecture of the St. Louis Fair," *Scribner's* 35 (April 1904); Frances H. Stadler, ed., *The Louisiana Purchase Exposition* (St. Louis: Missouri Historical Society, 1979); C. Howard Walker, "The Louisiana Purchase Exposition at St. Louis, Missouri," *Architectural Review* 11 (August 1904): 197–220.

5. This decision probably was made jointly by Gilbert and Masqueray. Cass Gilbert to Emmanuel Masqueray, May 2, 1902, Louisiana Purchase Letterbook, Cass Gilbert Collection, N-YHS.

6. These two buildings were the ones he most coveted. On September 11, 1901, Isaac Taylor, director of works, had written: "Name two [or] three buildings from which you would like to have one, and we will see if you cannot be pleased." Taylor to Cass Gilbert, September 11, 1901, Box 14, File 100, Cass Gilbert Collection, MHS. Each architect was to receive a $10,000 honorarium in addition to traveling expenses, drafting costs, and supplies. Thomas Hastings, in particular, was angered that Gilbert got the commission for the Palace of Fine Arts. See John R. Rachac, September 21, 1901, Notes, Box 14, File 100, Cass Gilbert Papers, MHS, and Isaac Taylor to Cass Gilbert, September 21, 1901, Box 14, File 100, Cass Gilbert Collection, Manuscripts Division, LofC. See also Pamela Hemenway, "Cass Gilbert's Buildings at the Louisiana Purchase Exposition, 1904" (master's thesis, University of Missouri, Columbia, 1970).

7. In 1915 Gilbert explored the possibility of expanding the Art Museum in St. Louis. Two proposals that draw on the early designs of 1901 are held at the New-York Historical Society. The expansion did not take place, although Gilbert did remodel three galleries in the east wing for use as a library.

8. Compare Festival Hall to the domed Petit Palais by Charles Girault, built to house French art at the Universal Exposition in Paris. The building featured oculus windows and stuccoed, vaulted ceilings, much like those of Gilbert's Festival Hall. For an illustration, see Philippe Jullian, *The Triumph of the Art Nouveau* (London: Phaidon, 1974), 48. The cascades in front of Festival Hall were the creation of Emmanuel Masqueray.

9. Folke Tyko Kihlstedt suggested that the prototype of the plan for Festival Hall was a Roman *caldarium*, particularly when considered in relation to the Art Building's Sculpture Hall, which probably imitated the *apodyterium* of a thermal bath. Kihlstedt, "Formal and Structural Innovations in American Exposition Architecture: 1901–1939" (Ph.D. diss., Northwestern University, Evanston, Ill., 1973), 83. Festival Hall was awarded a gold medal for architecture by the exposition judges.

10. For a good six months after receiving the commission for the Art Building in September 1901, Cass Gilbert was stymied by the Exposition Company's uncertainty regarding the building program. In November of 1901, the Commission of Architects decided that a monumental "point" at the top of the hill, on the main axis, was necessary. The Art Building, slated for the hilltop, would have been too expensive if lavished with ornament as the commission thought proper. It was decided that the Art Building would be screened by the temporary Festival Hall. Cass Gilbert to Isaac Taylor, November 13, 1901, Louisiana Purchase Letterbook, July 1901–January 1904, Cass Gilbert Collection, N-YHS; Isaac W. Morton to Isaac Taylor, November 30, 1901, Louisiana Purchase Letterbook, Cass Gilbert Collection, N-YHS.

11. The permanent central portion, the Art Building, was erected at a cost of $945,000. See Gerald Baum, "The Park Art Building: How It Came to Be," 31, unpublished paper in St. Louis Art Museum Archives.

12. Personifications of Classic, Renaissance, Gothic, Asian, Egyptian, and Modern art stand upon the cornice in front of the arched window that lights

the main sculpture gallery. At each end of the main building, pairs of Ionic columns flank niches that contained figures of gilded staff, Truth and Nature. Two-thirds of the way up the limestone wall, encircling three faces of the building, a pilastrade features carved screens alternating with medallion portraits of famous artists.

13. See Arthur Drexler, ed., *The Architecture of the Ecole des Beaux-Arts* (New York: Museum of Modern Art, 1977), 240–41.

14. Many of his sketches are contained in the Prints and Drawings Collection of Avery Architectural and Fine Arts Library, Columbia University, New York City. See also "Studies and Sketches for the Festival Hall, Louisiana Purchase Exposition," *Architectural Review* 11 (May 1904): plates 23–24.

15. Halsey Cooley Ives to Cass Gilbert, November 29, 1901, on behalf of the Committee of Directors, Department of Art, Louisiana Purchase Exposition, MoHS. Ives noted that the Chicago Fine Arts Building had 15,700 linear feet for displays compared to the Art Building at St. Louis with 7,126 feet. I thank Joan Draper for including my paper "Cass Gilbert, Halsey Cooley Ives, and the St. Louis Art Museum" in an open session of the Society of Architectural Historians, Pittsburgh, April 1985. Thanks go, as well, to the St. Louis Chapter of the American Institute of Architects for inviting me to explore these ideas further with them in October 1991 in my unpublished lecture "Perpetual Discovery and the St. Louis Art Museum."

16. Osmund Overby cited the Baths of Caracalla and the Basilica of Maxentius as prototypes for the St. Louis schemes. See Overby, "The Saint Louis Art Museum: An Architectural History," *Saint Louis Art Museum Bulletin* 18 (fall 1987): 8. The parallel is reiterated by Hugh Hardy in Hardy Holzman Pfeiffer Associates and James N. Wood, *The Architecture of the St. Louis Art Museum, 1904–1977* (St. Louis: St. Louis Art Museum, 1977).

17. Gilbert resigned from the Commission of Architects in the spring of 1904 and sued the Louisiana Purchase Exposition Company for $47,113.04. Gilbert's initial scheme for the Art Building had been rejected, and he claimed that the company had broken the contract when they requested a redesign. The Art Building was then screened by Festival Hall. The judge of the U.S. Circuit Court decided in Gilbert's favor in March 1905, but reduced his award. See Journal, March 27, 1905, 247, Cass Gilbert Collection, N-YHS, and *American Architect and Building News* 84 (May 14, 1904): 53.

18. Cass Gilbert to Julia Finch Gilbert, March 30, 1905, Box 7, 1905 file, Cass Gilbert Collection, Manuscript Division, LofC.

19. See Dana Cuff, *Architecture: The Story of Practice* (Cambridge, Mass.: M.I.T. Press, 1991): 91ff.

20. Drawings for University of Minnesota schemes are held in the University Archives of the University of Minnesota (Walter Library) in Minneapolis and at the Northwest Architectural Archives in St. Paul. See Michael Conforti, ed., *Minnesota 1900: Art and Life on the Upper Mississippi, 1890–1915* (Newark, Del.: University of Delaware Press, 1994). Gilbert became involved in planning projects for New York City in 1923 as chairman of a committee of architects who were to explore solutions to congestion in the area around City Hall Park. They also proposed an overall plan for Manhattan. For more information on this complicated story, see David A. Johnson, *Planning the Great Metropolis: The 1929 Regional Plan of New York and Its Environs* (New York: E. & F. N. Spon, 1996).

21. Frederick Norton Finney, a railroad magnate from St. Louis, honored his father, Charles Grandison Finney, a former president of Oberlin College, with a chapel to replace the recently burned one. The president of Oberlin, Henry Churchill King, contacted Gilbert at Finney's request as early as December 1903. King to Cass Gilbert, December 15, 1903, Incoming Oberlin Correspondence, Cass Gilbert Collection, N-YHS. In Gilbert's "Report," March 16, 1904, 2, he mentioned that his own father had been a student at Oberlin. Gilbert Collection, N-YHS. See also Geoffrey Blodgett, *Oberlin College Architecture: A Short History* (Oberlin, Ohio: Oberlin College, 1979), and Blodgett, "President King and Cass Gilbert: The Grand Collaboration," *Oberlin Alumni Magazine* 79 (winter 1983): 15–19. On Finney Chapel, see Blodgett's pamphlet *Finney Chapel* (Oberlin, Ohio: Office of College Information, 1973). Thanks to Professor Blodgett for sharing his work with me.

22. This letter, dated January 22, 1905, reads in part: "[Archbishop Ireland] and I promenaded the corridors [of the Minnesota Capitol] alone for an hour then sat in the commissioners [sic] room for an hour and talked Cathedral. He tried to induce me to enter the Cathedral competition. I *declined* though partly tempted to do so." Cass Gilbert to Julia Gilbert, January 22, 1905, Box 7, Cass Gilbert Collection, Manuscript Division, LofC.

23. The facade of Finney Chapel somewhat resembles that of St. Gilles-du-Gard, a twelfth-century abbey church. This French medieval example was admired by Stanford White as well. See Leland M. Roth, *McKim, Mead and White, Architects* (New York: Harper and Row, 1983), 53.

24. Cass Gilbert to Henry Churchill King, April 23, 1906, Oberlin Letterbook, Cass Gilbert Collection, N-YHS.

25. George H. Wells to S. C. Gladwin, December 31, 1907, and Cass Gilbert to Gladwin, January 7, 1908, Oberlin Letterbook, Cass Gilbert Collection, N-YHS.

26. Cass Gilbert to Charles Williams, February 27, 1908, Oberlin Letterbook, Cass Gilbert Collection, N-YHS.

27. In addition to the chapel and the art building, Gilbert also designed the hospital, although his son, Cass Gilbert Jr., was primarily responsible for the 1924 design, now much altered. An Oberlin staff member recalled: "A luncheon was given in his [Cass Gilbert's] honor with faculty and important citizens attending. One woman sitting next to a friend began telling what was wrong with the buildings, ending, 'You can't see anything in the Art Building, you can't hear any-

thing in the Chapel, but you can hear everything in the Hospital.' Imagine how she felt when the man on her right was introduced as Cass Gilbert!" Frances Yocum to Betty and Don Irish, January 25, 1985, collection of the author.

28. For a good summary of Gilbert's involvements at Oberlin College, see Arnold W. Klukas and Margarita J. Wuellner, "'Beauty, Utility, and Fitness': Cass Gilbert in Oberlin," in *Building Utopia: Oberlin Architecture, 1833–1983/Bulletin of the Allen Memorial Art Museum* 41, no. 1 (1983–84): 35–42. See also the thirty-one-page report by the Olmsted Brothers addressed to H. C. King, June 20, 1903, Oberlin College Archives, Oberlin, Ohio.

29. For a description of the Allen Memorial Art Building with ample illustrations and plans, see I. T. Frary, "The Dudley Peter Allen Memorial Art Building, Oberlin, Ohio," *Architectural Record* 44 (August 1918): 98–112. See also Robert Venturi, "Plain and Fancy Architecture by Cass Gilbert at Oberlin," *Apollo* 103 (February 1976): 86–89, and Venturi, "Plain and Fancy Architecture by Cass Gilbert at Oberlin and an Addition to the Museum by Venturi and Rauch," *Oberlin College Bulletin* 34 (1976–77): 83–104.

30. For a good analysis of this building see Charles Savage, *The Rodin Studio Art Building* (New York: New York Landmarks Preservation Commission, 1988).

31. For more illustrations and plans, see "Cass Gilbert's 200 West 57th Street Studio Building," *American Architect and Building News* 113 (January 9, 1918): 38, 41, plates.

32. See Christopher Tunnard, "A City Called Beautiful," *Journal of the Society of Architectural Historians* 9 (March/May 1950): 35.

33. To build the new library, David Hoadley's nineteenth-century Bristol House was demolished. Gilbert salvaged the carved wooden arches and moved them to the dining room of his country house in Ridgefield, Connecticut. The front doorway of Bristol House is in the Metropolitan Museum of Art. Jeanne Timpanelli, "Education Committee News," *Tavern Times,* autumn 1984, unpaginated. See also Peter Slatin, "First Addition: New Haven Free Public Library Renovation and Expansion," *Architectural Record,* January 1992, 90–97. Hugh Hardy of Hardy Holzman Pfeiffer called the Ives Memorial Library at New Haven an "overgrown English country house" (93). His firm has recently renovated and enlarged Gilbert's building.

34. John R. Rockart, I. D. Waterman, and C. W. Lord, "The Relation of Buildings, Retaining Walls and Bridges, and their Surroundings to City Development," in *The Relations of Railways to City Development* (Washington, D.C.: American Institute of Architects, 1909), 48.

35. An addition to the station was built in 1954 by the Detroit firm of Yamasaki, Leinweber and Associates. It has recently been restored. Gilbert's station continued the dialogue that he had maintained with the office of McKim, Mead and White. The New Haven station shares compositional features with the central brick block of the New York, New Haven and Hartford Railroad Station in Waterbury, Connecticut

(1906–9), designed by a partner in the McKim, Mead and White firm, William Symmes Richardson. For more on the Waterbury station, see Roth, *McKim, Mead and White,* 341. Carroll L. V. Meeks in *The Railroad Station: An Architectural History* (New Haven: Yale University Press, 1956), 130–31, noted similarities among the St. Louis Fair's Transportation Building (E. Masqueray, 1904), Detroit's Michigan Central Station (Warren and Wetmore; Reed and Stem, 1913), and Gilbert's New Haven Station.

36. Rockart et al., "The Relation of Buildings," 48.

37. The six stations included Hunts Point, Port Morris, Westchester Avenue, and Pelham Manor. In addition to the illustrated article by Rockart et al., there are two other sources of information about these deteriorating stations, which were closed in 1937. See [Montgomery Schuyler], "Along the 'Harlem River Branch,'" *Architectural Record* 24 (December 1908): 417–29, and Christopher Gray, "Discarded Elegance Near the Point of No Return," *New York Times,* February 4, 1990, X:11. Carl Condit shared the latter article with me.

38. "Cass Gilbert Buys Old Tavern," *Democrat* (Madison, Wisc.), August 20, 1907, in Scrapbook, 1901–9, Cass Gilbert Collection, N-YHS. Also the Keeler Tavern Preservation Society in Ridgefield, Connecticut, produces a newsletter that has useful details about the Gilbert phase of the building.

39. Gilbert joined the Sons of the Revolution in 1898. See Cashbook 1898–1910, Cass Gilbert Collection, N-YHS. He joined the Ohio Society of New York in 1901. See Ledger January 1901–June 1905, Cass Gilbert Collection, N-YHS. See also Wallace E. Davies, *Patriotism on Parade: The Story of Veterans and Hereditary Organizations in America, 1783–1900* (Cambridge: Harvard University Press, 1956), and David C. Hammack, *Power and Society: Greater New York at the Turn of the Century* (New York: Russell Sage Foundation, 1982).

40. Cass Gilbert to Cass Gilbert Jr., January 29, 1929, Personal Letters, Cass Gilbert Collection, N-YHS.

41. I have explored a few possibilities in my article "Physical Spaces and Public Life," *Nordic Journal of Architectural Research* 4 (1994): 25–34.

42. Paul Clifford Larson, in *Minnesota Architect: The Life and Work of Clarence Howard Johnston* (Afton, Minn.: Afton Historical Society Press, 1996), 16–17, gives a thorough history of the New York Architectural Sketch Club, which became the Architectural League of New York.

43. Quoted by W. Francklyn Paris, "Cass Gilbert: Master Builder," *Hall of American Artists* 4 (1948): unpaginated. Three different presidents—Roosevelt, Taft, and Wilson—appointed Gilbert to the Council (later Commission) of Fine Arts. He was an honorary member of the Royal Institute of British Architects, the Royal Academy of Arts, and the Royal Architectural Institute of Canada. He was a chevalier of the Legion of Honor and helped to organize the American Society of the French Legion of Honor. He received honorary degrees from New York University, Oberlin College, Middlebury College, the University of Michigan, Princeton University,

and Columbia University. He was also a trustee of the Metropolitan Museum of Art, the Carnegie Institute of Washington, D.C., and the Pilgrim Society. He belonged to the Century Association and the Metropolitan Club, among others. See "Cass Gilbert Dead; Eminent Architect," *New York Times*, May 18, 1934, 25, and Guy Kirkham, "Cass Gilbert: Master of Style," *Pencil Points* 15 (November 1934): 541–56.

44. For an excellent summary of the growth of American public libraries and sources for further research, see Elizabeth Greenwell Grossman, *The Civic Architecture of Paul Cret* (Cambridge, Eng.: Cambridge University Press, 1996), 65–74.

45. For a good account of the Boston Public Library, see Leland Roth's *McKim, Mead and White, Architects*. For Carrère and Hastings's New York Public Library, see Robert A. M. Stern, Gregory Gilmartin, and John Massengale, *New York 1900: Metropolitan Architecture and Urbanism, 1890–1915* (New York: Rizzoli, 1983), 91–97. Cass Gilbert was appointed in 1897 to serve on the seven-member jury for the New York Public Library competition. John Carrère to Cass Gilbert, October 11, 1897, Box 18, Cass Gilbert Papers, MHS.

46. Six of the competition designs are illustrated in "The New Library Building," *Realty Record and Builder* 14 (July 1907): unpaginated, and four appear in the August 1907 issue of *Western Architect*. The competitors were Barnett, Haynes and Barnett; Carrère and Hastings; Eames and Young; William B. Ittner; Theodore Link; Mauran, Russell and Garden; Palmer and Hornbostel; and Albert K. Ross, in addition to Cass Gilbert. The jurors were Walter Cook of New York, Frank Miles Day of Philadelphia, and Philip Sawyer of New York, all chosen by polling the competitors. See also "The St. Louis Public Library Competition," *Brickbuilder* 16 (June 1907).

47. Cass Gilbert to Paul Blackwelder, October 11, 1907, St. Louis Public Library Letterbook, Cass Gilbert Collection, N-YHS. Blackwelder was the acting secretary of the St. Louis Public Library board and the assistant librarian.

48. In "New Library Building," the editors claimed that "the absence of columns will add very much to the beauty of the building" (unpaginated).

49. In the attic story, medallions carry signs of the zodiac, heads of gods and goddesses, an owl, an eagle, an hourglass, and seals of St. Louis and its library. Medallions on the entrance pavilion carry portrait heads of Homer, Dante, Virgil, and Shakespeare (left to right). Nine muses and three graces were carved in low relief and set into the jambs of the beveled arches. Thirty shields representing printers were carved on stone panels below the arched windows. Just below the main cornice appear incised names of famous authors. An undated commemorative pamphlet, "The Public Library of the City of St. Louis," contains many details about the building. I am grateful to David Van Zanten, who gave me this illustrated booklet.

50. The Steedman Architectural Library was added in 1930. The east inner court was filled in to

house a new children's literature room and a rare book room in 1968.

51. Although he was writing about state capitols, Gilbert emphasized the importance of educating the public with civic architecture in "The Greatest Element of Monumental Architecture," *American Architect* 136 (August 5, 1929): 143–44. He wrote: "The poor man can not fill his home with works of art. The State can, however, satisfy his natural craving for such things in the enjoyment of which all may freely share, by properly embellishing its public buildings."

52. "Ceilings are Artistic," *St. Louis Republic*, November 7, 1910, 17.

53. On Gilbert's campus plans at Texas, see Carol McMichael, *Paul Cret at Texas: Architectural Drawing and the Image of the University in the 1930s* (Austin: Archer M. Huntington Gallery, 1983). This is a well-illustrated and informative catalog. Barbara Christen, in "Cass Gilbert's Grand Vision of the American Campus, 1899–1915" (Ph.D. diss., Graduate Center, City University of New York, 1997), examines Gilbert's campus plans at Oberlin, Minnesota, and Texas, among others. An early scheme for Gilbert's campus plan at Austin appears on the back of a letter from his brother, Samuel Gilbert; Cass Gilbert Collection, Box 8, File 1911, Manuscripts Division, LofC.

54. Lawrence W. Speck noted "a 'golden era' of Mediterranean Classicism in the southern United States in the early decades of this century when the region's longstanding predilections became coincident with national and international architectural interests." See his "Comment," in *Center* 2 (1986): 5. This special issue, "Ah Mediterranean! Twentieth Century Classicism in America," was edited by Charles W. Moore and Wayne Attoe. It includes excellent color reproductions of Gilbert's buildings.

55. For a description of changes to Gilbert's two buildings, see Jeffrey Karl Ochsner, "The Renewal of Sutton Hall: Architecture Complex Taking Shape at UT-Austin," *Texas Architect* 33 (March/April 1983): 60–63. Lawrence W. Speck offers an appreciation of Battle Hall in "Timeliness and Timelessness," *Center* 2 (1986): 118–19.

56. For more information on the Detroit competition and the library building, consult Peter Federman's descriptive article "The Detroit Public Library," *Classical America* 4 (1977): 85–112; W. Francklyn Paris, "Italian Renaissance in Detroit," *American Architect* 123 (January 3, 1923): 15–19, 21; Paris, "The Mosaics in the Frontal Colonnade of the Detroit Public Library," *Architectural Record* 49 (April 1921): 301–9; and Frank B. Woodford, *Parnassus on Main Street* (Detroit: Wayne State University Press, 1965). Daniel Bluestone's "Detroit's City Beautiful and the Problem of Commerce," in *Journal of the Society of Architectural Historians* 47 (September 1988): 245–62, takes a look at the library in the context of the Center for Arts and Letters that was supposed to counterbalance the commercialism of Detroit.

57. Grossman, *Civic Architecture of Paul Cret*, 70. The program for the Detroit library was written by Philadelphia architect Frank Miles Day.

58. Elizabeth Grossman does an excellent job of "reading" this building and I am in her debt. Again, see her *Civic Architecture of Paul Cret*.

59. For a full description and illustrations of this project, see William A. Coles, "The History of America's Greatest Fountain: The Scott Memorial Fountain on Belle Isle, Detroit," *Classical America* 3 (1973): 5–26.

60. Many sketches for the Belle Isle bridge are held at the New York Historical Society. See also E. H. Bennett, *Preliminary Plan of Detroit together with Sketch Plans for a New Bridge to Belle Isle by Cass Gilbert, Architect; Barclay Parsons and Klapp, Engineers* (Detroit: City Plan and Improvement Commission, 1915).

CHAPTER 4

1. See Sharon Irish, "A 'Machine that Makes the Land Pay': The West Street Building in New York," *Technology and Culture* 30 (April 1989): 376–97.

2. Sources for the West Street Building's flamboyant detailing include the cathedral at Malines, Belgium, and Louvain's town hall.

3. John Starin (1825–1909) was a prominent member of the Holland Society of America. See Irish, "West Street Building," 378–79. Also see Michael Kammen, "The Rediscovery of New York's History, Phase One," *New York History* 60 (October 1979): 372–406.

4. A large drawing for an elaborate elevator screen is held in the Prints and Drawings Collection of the Avery Architectural and Fine Arts Library, Columbia University. See my forthcoming essay, "Cass Gilbert in Practice," in the catalog for the 2000 New-York Historical Society exhibition of Cass Gilbert's work.

5. For a complimentary essay on Gilbert's early skyscrapers, see [Montgomery Schuyler], "The West Street Building," *Architectural Record* 22 (August 1907): 103–9.

6. See the insightful essay on skylines by William R. Taylor, "New York and the Origin of the Skyline: The Commercial City as Visual Text," *In Pursuit of Gotham: Culture and Commerce in New York* (New York: Oxford University Press, 1992), 20–25.

7. For information about the general development of skyscrapers, see the excellent work by Sarah Bradford Landau and Carl W. Condit, *Rise of the New York Skyscraper, 1865–1913* (New Haven: Yale University Press, 1996). The authors provide a fine bibliography. For a concise, useful summary of the history of the skyscraper, see John Tauranac's chapter on the subject in *The Empire State Building: The Making of a Landmark* (New York: Scribner's, 1995). Carol Willis's *Form Follows Finance: Skyscrapers and Skylines in New York and Chicago* (New York: Princeton Architectural Press, 1995) takes a broad view of developments in New York and Chicago from the late nineteenth century up through the 1940s. Willis, too, provides a helpful bibliography.

8. Frank Winfield Woolworth founded his company in Lancaster, Pennsylvania, in 1879. By 1880, his idea of pricing every item in his store at five or ten cents had paid off. By adding partners and stores, Woolworth soon had a large business that was incorporated as the F. W. Woolworth Compa-ny on December 15, 1911. For more on Woolworth, see James Brough, *The Woolworths* (New York: McGraw Hill, 1982); John P. Nichols, *Skyline Queen and Merchant Prince* (New York: Trident Press, 1973); and John K. Winkler, *Five and Ten* (New York: Robert M. McBride, 1940). An era of retailing ended in 1997 when the Woolworth Company announced the closure of its five-and-dime stores. Jennifer Steinhauer, "Woolworth Gives Up on the Five-and-Dime," *New York Times,* July 18, 1997, 1.

9. Initially Woolworth planned to build on the southwest corner of Broadway and Park Place. Gilbert and his team tried four schemes for a smaller building before more property was acquired. Late in 1910, Woolworth purchased the adjacent lot so that the frontage extended along Broadway from Park Place to Barclay Street.

10. Diary of Cass Gilbert, 1897–98, General Correspondence, Cass Gilbert Collection, Manuscripts Division, LofC.

11. Carol Willis, in *Form Follows Finance*, 45, claims that the Woolworth Building was known as a "poor performer" in the real-estate market.

12. Contemporary publications on the Woolworth Building abound. In *Brickbuilder*, see "New Woolworth Building" 19 (November 1910): 261–62. Gunvald Aus and Cass Gilbert wrote about the Woolworth's engineering in *American Architect* 103 (March 26, 1913): 157–70. *Engineering Record* published periodic updates on the building: May 27, 1911; August 26, 1911; February 17, 1912; February 24, 1912; April 27, 1912; June 29, 1912; July 27, 1912; July 5, 1913; July 12, 1913; July 26, 1913; and September 5, 1914. Many excellent illustrations can be found in "The Woolworth Building," a promotional brochure by Edward Hogan published in New York in 1912. George T. Mortimer discusses "Building Equipment and Management—The Woolworth Building" in *Real Estate Magazine*, July 1912, 52–69, a well-illustrated article. "The Tallest Office Building in the World: Erection of the Woolworth Building, New York" appeared in *Scientific American* 108 (March 8, 1913): 224–25, 233. "Shooting Streams from the Woolworth's Pinnacle: Practical Fire Test of Standpipe System in the World's Tallest Building," appeared in *Fire and Water Engineering* 53 (June 11, 1913): 384–86. Montgomery Schuyler wrote *The Woolworth Building,* a booklet published privately in New York in 1913. Schuyler also wrote "The Towers of Manhattan and Notes on the Woolworth Building," *Architectural Record* 33 (February 1913): 98–122. G. Leland Hunter wrote "Notes on Gargoyles, Grotesques and Chimeras," for *Architectural Record* 35 (1914): 132–39. See "Frame and Windbracing of the Woolworth Building," *Engineering News* 72, no. 5 (July 30, 1914): 231–33. Clarence Ward assessed the Woolworth Tower in *American Magazine of Art*, December 1916, 54–60. Edwin A. Cochran's *The Cathedral of Commerce, the Highest Building in the World* (Baltimore: Thomsen-Ellis, 1918) has an introduction by S. Parkes Cadman. The F. W. Woolworth Company celebrated its history in *Fifty Years of Woolworth, 1879–1929* (New York, 1929). Some of Gilbert's own comments on the

Woolworth Tower appear in Julia Finch Gilbert, ed., *Cass Gilbert: Reminiscences and Addresses* (New York: Scribner Press, 1935). In addition to many brief mentions in other periodicals and newspapers, there is a growing literature on the Woolworth Company Building. Howard F. Koeper's Ph.D. diss., "The Gothic Skyscraper" (Harvard University, Cambridge, Mass., 1969) is a good place to start. See also Robert Allen Jones, "Mr. Woolworth's Tower: The Skyscraper as Popular Icon," *Journal of Popular Culture* 7 (fall 1973): 408–24. Donald M. Reynolds wrote "The Tallest Building in the World, 1913–30," in *Immovable Objects* (New York: Cooper-Hewitt Museum, 1975), 4, and devoted a chapter to the Woolworth Building in his *Architecture of New York City* (New York: MacMillan, 1984). See also Spencer Klaw's "The World's Tallest Building," *American Heritage* 28 (February 1977): 87–99. John Zukowsky published "Cathedrals of Commerce" in *American Art and Antiques*, January/February 1979, 106–13. Robert A. M. Stern, Gregory Gilmartin, and John Massengale, in *New York 1900: Metropolitan Architecture and Urbanism, 1890–1915* (New York: Rizzoli, 1983), also discuss the Woolworth Building and provide a bibliography. "Woolworth's Cathedral" by John Steele Gordon appeared in *American Heritage* 10 (July/August 1988): 16ff. See also Gail Fenske and Deryck Holdsworth, "Corporate Identity and the New York Office Building: 1895–1915," in *The Landscape of Modernity: Essays on New York City, 1900–1940,* ed. David Ward and Olivier Zunz (New York: Russell Sage Foundation, 1992), 129–59. Gail Fenske's Ph.D. diss., "The 'Skyscraper Problem' and the City Beautiful: The Woolworth Building" (M.I.T., Cambridge, Mass., 1988), is being revised for publication. For an excellent summary of the Woolworth Building in the context of other New York skyscrapers, see Landau and Condit, *Rise of the New York Skyscraper.*

13. Cass Gilbert, "Tenth Birthday of a Notable Structure," *Real Estate Magazine* 11 (May 1923): 344–45, as cited in Fenske and Holdsworth, "Corporate Identity," 158 n.41.

14. A conversation between Frank Woolworth and Cass Gilbert about the building's height was reported by Charles W. Person, "New York's Greatest Lighting Spectacle," *Scientific American* 112, no. 8 (February 20, 1915): 171. The seven-hundred-foot-high Metropolitan Life tower (1907–9) was designed by Pierre L. Lebrun of Napoleon Lebrun and Sons.

15. The steel was shipped via the Pennsylvania Railroad from the American Bridge Company in Pittsburgh and then was transferred to a lighter at a Manhattan pier before being trucked to the site. Delivery routes had to be tested to see if the streets could bear the load of the massive quantity of materials. Safety measures for workers and pedestrians and communications systems on- and off-site were devised on a scale never before needed. Hoisting, mixing, and handling of materials were all mechanized.

16. The Atlantic Terracotta Company had the contract for the Woolworth Building's terra-cotta cladding; the sculptors, John Donnelly and Eliseo Ricci, did the designs. The terra-cotta units were attached to their brick backings with metal anchors. Margaret F. Gaskie reported on "The Woolworth Tower: A Technology Revisited," in *Architectural Record,* mid-August 1981, 90–95; also see Reynolds, *Architecture of New York City,* 170–73.

17. See also Ann Douglas, *The Feminization of American Culture* (New York: Avon Books, 1977), 78: "Advertising was more than a business . . . it involved a way of life and a theory of human nature."

18. Landau and Condit, *Rise of the New York Skyscraper,* 387, and Gail Fenske, telephone conversation with author, 1997. "Remember, please, that the skyscraper is not designed from the standpoint of a monument alone or of a church tower, but from the standpoint of a business use, for the purpose of producing rent and profit," Gilbert insisted in 1931 when he received a gold medal from the Society of Arts and Sciences. "Response on Occasion of the Receipt of the Gold Medal from the Society of Arts and Sciences," in Julia Finch Gilbert, *Reminiscences and Addresses,* 6.

19. Thomas C. Cochran and William Miller, *The Age of Enterprise: A Social History of Industrial America* (New York: Harper Torchbooks, 1961), 230.

20. William R. Taylor, in "The Evolution of Public Space: The Commercial City as Showcase," *In Pursuit of Gotham,* 31, notes that Woolworth "based his success on the close observation of consumer habits of ordinary people."

21. Thirty-three heads ornament the keystones of the first-floor windows at the Library of Congress. See Herbert Small, *The Library of Congress: Its Architecture and Decoration* (New York: Classical America, 1982), 37–40. Heads on keystones above the second-floor windows along the east and west sides of the Custom House included these "types": Caucasian, Hindu, Latin, Celt, Mongolian, Eskimo, Slav, and African. The sculptor was V. Alfano. On the Woolworth Building, the heads, from south to north, may represent Africa, America, Europe, and Asia. See Anthony W. Robins, *The Woolworth Building* (New York: Landmarks Preservation Commission, 1983).

22. Thanks go to architect Garth Rockcastle for pointing this out to me during a seminar at the University of Minnesota. William R. Taylor and Thomas Bender make this point as well in "Culture and Architecture: Some Aesthetic Tensions in the Shaping of New York," *In Pursuit of Gotham,* 41.

23. Edwin Blashfield to Cass Gilbert, August 5, 1907, Cass Gilbert Collection, Manuscripts Division, LofC.

24. There is not space to explore this topic here, but Gilbert's fascination with his own heritage and his involvement with organizations like Sons of the American Revolution and the Anglo-Saxon movement as well as his frequent visits to England add a dimension to his watercolors and his architectural designs that is worth exploring further. Gilbert had a nostalgia for the American colonial era, wanted to balance urban, commercial designs with rural, pre-industrial landscapes (often in painting), and attempted to infuse

modern urban structures with selected Anglo-American elements. See Geoffrey Blodgett, "Cass Gilbert, Architect: Conservative at Bay," *Journal of American History* 72 (December 1985): 615–36; Michael A. Lutzker, "The Practical Peace Advocates: An Interpretation of the American Peace Movement, 1898–1917" (Ph.D. diss., Rutgers University, New Brunswick, N.J., 1969); and William B. Rhoads, "The Colonial Revival and the Americanization of Immigrants," in *The Colonial Revival in America,* ed. Alan Axelrod (New York: W. W. Norton, 1985), 341–61.

25. Cass Gilbert to Julia Gilbert, August 1, 1906, Box 7, Cass Gilbert Collection, Manuscript Division, LofC.

26. See John Clubbe, *Cincinnati Observed: Architecture and History* (Columbus: Ohio State University Press, 1992).

27. Robert A. M. Stern, Gregory Gilmartin, and Thomas Mellins, in *New York 1930: Architecture and Urbanism between the Two World Wars* (New York: Rizzoli, 1987), provide a useful assessment of the building complexes at Foley Square.

28. See Phyllis A. Zimmerman, *The Neck of the Bottle: George W. Goethals and the Reorganization of the U.S. Army Supply System, 1917–18* (College Station, Tex.: Texas A&M University Press, 1992).

29. Because there was no centrally located rail terminal, it was cheaper and faster in New York harbor to transfer goods by car ferry and lighter than it was to rely on railroad-switching operations alone.

30. Warehouse A was 980 by 200 feet and Warehouse B was 980 by 300 feet. My forthcoming article on the Brooklyn military terminal will assess this project in depth, including the engineering associated with it. One engineer in particular, Arthur Newell Talbot, was a pioneer in materials science at the University of Illinois, Urbana-Champaign. There is ample literature on the Brooklyn Terminal in contemporary journals. See, for example: "Asphalt-Block Handling at Army Base" and "Paving of Streets and Aisles, Brooklyn Army Supply Base," *Engineering News-Record* 83 (August 28, 1919): 400–402, 439; "Army Supply Base, Brooklyn," *Builder* 119 (December 24, 1920): 719; P. Calfas, "Entrepôts Militaires du Port de New-York: La 'base' de Brooklyn," *Le génie civil* 74 (May 17, 1919): 385–91; "Freight Handling at the Brooklyn Army Base," *Engineering News-Record* 83 (September 18, 1919): 555–60; Cass Gilbert, "Architecture of Industrial Building in Concrete," *Architectural Forum* 39 (September 1923): 83–86; Gilbert, "U.S. Army Supply Base, Brooklyn, New York," *American Architect* 116 (November 26, 1919): 651–60; George C. Nimmons, "Modern Industrial Plants: Part V. The Great Army Supply Bases and Quartermasters' Terminals of the United States Government," *Architectural Record* 45 (March 1919): 262–82; and "U.S. Army Supply Base," *Architectural Review,* n.s., 10 (1920): 1–4. Two other documents that provide substantial information are the nomination form of the National Register for the Brooklyn Terminal and the "Proposal for the Renovation of the Brooklyn Army Terminal," prepared in 1985 by the New York City Public Development Corporation.

31. The chairman of the Emergency Construction Committee of the War Industries Board, William Aiken Starrett, was a leader in the construction field. He worked with the construction quartermaster of the U.S. Army. Together, they worked with Gilbert; the contractor, Henry C. Turner; and the engineers, S. F. Holtzman and Kort Berle of the Aus Company. (Aus had retired in 1915.) For a general history of this time period see Zimmerman, *Neck of the Bottle.*

32. See *A Record of War Activities* (New York: Turner Construction Co., 1918), 88. This useful publication is available in the Turner Company offices in New York City.

33. See Federico Bucci, *Albert Kahn: Architect of Ford* (New York: Princeton Architectural Press, 1991), and Grant Hildebrand, *Designing for Industry: The Architecture of Albert Kahn* (Cambridge, Mass.: M.I.T. Press, 1974).

34. Moritz Kahn, *The Design and Construction of Industrial Buildings* (London: Technical Journals Ltd., 1917), cited in Bucci, 71 n.42.

35. A decade later, in 1928–29, Gilbert's designs informed those of Albert Kahn, as can be seen in Kahn's Fisher Building in Detroit, a variation on the American Perpendicular of Gilbert's New York Life Insurance Company Building. See Albert Kahn, "The Fisher Building," *American Architect* 135 (February 20, 1929): 211–44.

36. To date, I have more questions than answers about large-scale concrete construction. Toxement, a gray powder added to the concrete, was used to lubricate the aggregate and allow the cement to be chuted long distances. This substance was used on the Woolworth Building's foundations as well. Cass Gilbert to Turner Construction Company, August 31, 1918, Brooklyn Army Terminal Letterbook, Cass Gilbert Collection, N-YHS. I am grateful to those present at my talk to the Civil Engineering and Building Technology Interest Group (of the Society for the History of Technology) in Madison, Wisconsin, October 1991, who helped me frame questions I might pursue. On the Turner Construction Company see A. W. Chapman, "Brief History of the Turner Construction Company," *Turner Constructor* 4 (May 1927): 7–19.

37. See Claude Allen Porter Turner, *Concrete-Steel Construction* (Minneapolis: Farnham Printing and Stationery Company, 1909).

38. Warehouse B is divided into eight sections by movement joints, and lateral stability comes from the concrete facades and fire walls that run perpendicular to the facades.

39. The terminal's warehouses nevertheless caught the attention of modernist architects and writers. See, for example, Le Corbusier's aerial illustration of the buildings in *Towards a New Architecture* (New York: Frederick A. Praeger, 1946) and Richard Neutra's *Amerika: Die Stilbildung des neuen Bauens in den Vereinigten Staaten* (Vienna, 1930). On more recent changes, see Peter Slatin, "Renovating the Brooklyn Army Terminal," *Metropolis,* March 1989, 23–24.

40. File Memo "The Brooklyn Army Supply Base," December 30, 1919, Cass Gilbert Collection, N-YHS.

41. See Claude Bragdon, "Skyscrapers," *American Mercury* 22 (March 1931): 288–95. See also Stern et al., *New York 1930*, 541–44, where this building is analyzed; the authors also offer a bibliography.

42. See "Madison Square Garden: An Account of the Passing of One of New York City's Architectural Landmarks," *American Architect* 128 (December 20, 1925): 513–24.

43. The remaining three stories at the top seem to be entirely devoted to utilities and corridors. I am indebted to Carl W. Condit for sharing his notes and bibliography with me. The entire issue of *American Architect* 135 (March 20, 1929) is about the New York Life Insurance Building.

44. "A Bridge of Naked Steel," editorial, *New York Times*, September 9, 1931, 26; see also "A Monumental Bridge," *Scientific American* 37 (November 1927): 418–20.

45. See citations above, Chapter 3, on the New Haven Library, and "Two Buildings at Waterbury, Connecticut," *Architectural Forum* 32 (March 1920): 111–12, plates 43–48. See also "Municipal Building at Waterbury, Connecticut," *American Architect* 108 (December 15, 1915): 384–91. Probably written by Gilbert, the commentary noted: "These forefathers of a great republic built with dignity, and with the reverence for good principles in the art of architecture that resulted in a type of Georgian architecture" (385).

46. Other views of the Chase Company and of Waterbury emerge in the Brass Workers History Project, *Brass Valley: The Story of Working People's Lives and Struggles in an American Industrial Region*, ed. Jeremy Brecher, Jerry Lombardi, and Jan Stackhouse (Philadelphia: Temple University Press, 1982).

47. For more on Anglo-Saxonism, see Helen Elizabeth Knuth, "The Climax of American Anglo-Saxonism, 1898–1905" (Ph.D. diss., Northwestern University, Evanston, Ill., 1958).

48. For a beautifully illustrated and thorough discussion of the United States Supreme Court building and its site, see Allan Greenberg and Stephen Kieran, "The United States Supreme Court Building, Washington, D.C.," *Antiques Magazine* (October 1985): 760–69. Also see Cass Gilbert Jr., "The United States Supreme Court Building," *Architecture* 72 (December 1935): 300–334. This article also contains many illustrations.

49. Several sources note that Henry Bacon, who had prepared one scheme for the Supreme Court prior to his death in 1924, probably based his ideas on an 1824 Ecole des Beaux-Arts project by Théodore Labrouste. Gilbert, in turn, adapted Bacon's Beaux-Arts design for his version of the building, combining it with ideas from Henri Labrouste's "Tribunal de cassation" (1824), the winning entry to the Prix de Rome competition. See Greenberg and Kieran, "United States Supreme Court Building," 762, 764–65, 767. For Henri Labrouste's scheme, see Arthur Drexler, ed., *The Architecture of the Ecole des Beaux-Arts* (New York: Museum of Modern Art, 1977), 156–58. On the Labrouste brothers and their generation, see David Van Zanten, *Designing Paris: The Architecture of Duban, Labrouste, Duc and Vaudoyer* (Cambridge, Mass.:

M.I.T. Press, 1987). Leland Roth suggested that Leo von Klenze's Glyptothek in Munich also might have been a model for Gilbert's Supreme Court Building. See Leland M. Roth, *McKim, Mead and White, Architects* (New York: Harper and Row, 1983), 343. Jefferson's Virginia State Capitol (1785) had been enlarged between 1904 and 1906 by the addition of wings to each side. Jefferson's initial capitol design as well as the addition certainly could have influenced Gilbert too.

50. For an unfavorable review of the Supreme Court Building, see William Harlan Hale, "The Grandeur That Is Washington," *Harper's Magazine* 168 (April 1934): 560–69. Hale concluded: "The buildings of the newer Washington may seem artificial and false; but are they not a true reflection of the age that produced them?" (569).

51. The east-west axis of the Supreme Court Building is aligned with the entrance to the Senate wing of the Capitol across the street.

52. Draperies were added later to ameliorate the poor acoustics and cut off the light coming in from the courtyards.

CONCLUSION

1. "Sometimes I will confess the thought has been in my mind to call in some of the young fellows like Holyoke, Haskell, Rockart, or Wells who have been with me for so many years and make a regular partnership, but [my temperament] has always deterred me from doing so." Cass Gilbert to Henry Rutgers Marshall, undated, General Correspondence, Box 7, 1905 file, Cass Gilbert Collection, Manuscript Division, LofC. Also to his son, Gilbert wrote that "I can never do my best work when I have to consider what an 'associate' wants me to do or say." Cass Gilbert to Cass Gilbert Jr., June 28, 1925, Personal Letters, Cass Gilbert Collection, N-YHS.

2. Cass Gilbert to E. S. J. Phillips, March 5, 1927, Box 12, Cass Gilbert Collection, Manuscript Division, LofC.

3. Cass Gilbert to Francis H. Bacon, July 25, 1927, Box 12, Cass Gilbert Collection, Manuscripts Division, LofC.

4. Excerpted from Ralph Waldo Emerson's "Lectures and Biographical Sketches," in *The American Transcendentalists: Their Prose and Poetry*, ed. Perry Miller (Garden City, N.Y.: Doubleday Anchor Books, 1957), 307.

5. This canon has its limitations, of course. Diane Ghirardo discusses a "hierarchy of taste that excludes more than it includes . . . [A] certain strata of society and a certain group of architects decide to evaluate a limited body of buildings according to a set of standards they then define." Ghirardo, "Introduction," *Out of Site: A Social Criticism of Architecture*, ed. Diane Ghirardo (Seattle: Bay Press, 1991), 11–12.

6. Donald Drew Egbert discusses the relationship between eclecticism and American individualism in "Foreign Influences in American Art," in *Foreign Influences in American Life: Essays and Critical Bibliographies*, ed. David F. Bowers (Princeton: Princeton University Press, 1944), 99–125.

SELECTED BUILDINGS

This list represents a work in progress, but it is useful to have a starting place. Much remains to be done in the study of Gilbert's career, especially after the Woolworth Company Building. I am indebted to Patricia Murphy's master's thesis (University of Virginia, 1979) on Gilbert's career prior to 1896. It has been difficult to verify some of the dates given here, but whenever possible, they reflect the building records. I excluded any works previously identified as Gilbert buildings if I had not yet found documentation for them in the office records. I included works by the firm of Gilbert and Taylor, which was in practice from 1885 to 1891. Not all of Gilbert's houses, depots, and churches have been included; some monuments, tombs, and stables have also been eliminated. An asterisk (*) indicates that the building is illustrated in this book.

Canada
ONTARIO
Ottawa
United States Legation, 1928–32

United States of America
ARKANSAS
Little Rock
Arkansas State Capitol (with George R. Mann), 1917

CONNECTICUT
Bridgeport
Bridgeport Peoples Savings Bank, 1916–18; addition, 1930

Lakeville
Maria H. Hotchkiss School, chapel, 1920; dormitories, 1922–23, 1926–27; infirmary, 1927

New Haven
*Ives Memorial Library, 1908–11
*New York, New Haven and Hartford Railroad Station (now called Union Station), 1909–18

Waterbury
*Chase Manufacturing Company Offices, 1917–19; dispensary, 1923–24
*Municipal Building, 1914–15
Waterbury National Bank, 1920–21
*Waterbury Club, 1917–18

Waterford
Seaside Employees Home and Sanatorium, 1932–34

MASSACHUSETTS
Beverly
Library, 1911–13

Boston
*Brazer Building, 1896–97
Suffolk Savings Bank, 1905 (demolished)

MICHIGAN
Detroit
*Detroit Public Library, 1913–21
*James Scott Memorial Fountain, Belle Isle, 1921–22

MINNESOTA
Anoka
*Great Northern Railroad Depot, 1891

Duluth
Board of Trade, 1885 (demolished)
St. Louis Hotel, 1901

Faribault
Shattuck School, armory and library, 1910

Little Falls
Great Northern Railroad Depot, 1899

Minneapolis
Federal Reserve Bank, 1921–25
Minneapolis and St. Louis Railroad Depot, 1891
Realty Company Storage Warehouse, 1903
Western Cities Trust Company Building, 1900

Minnetonka
Camp Memorial Chapel, 1888

Moorhead
*St. John the Divine Episcopal Church, 1898–99

St. Cloud
C. D. Kerr Store Building, 1888

St. Paul
J. Q. Adams Houses, 1884–88 (demolished)
E. H. Bailey House, 1889
Mrs. J. W. Bass House, 1891
R. B. C. Bement House, 1888–89
*Bookstaver Row Houses (Portland Terrace), 1888
Boston and Northwest Real Estate Company Warehouse and Offices, 1893–94
Boston Clothing House Block, 1895 (demolished)
Bowlby Building, 1895
Stiles Burr House, 1899
Sylvester Cary House, 1888
E. D. Chamberlin Building, 1896
Clark House, 1889
*Dayton Avenue Presbyterian Church, 1886; additions, 1902, 1909–10, 1911
William J. Dean House, 1894
Jacob Dittenhofer House, 1898
Howard N. Elmer House, 1890
*Endicott Building, 1889–91; renovation, 1916
Galusha Row Houses, 1887
*German Bethlehem Presbyterian Church, 1890
Cass Gilbert House, 1889
*Elizabeth Wheeler Gilbert House, 1882–84
*Paul Gotzian House, 1889
*Gotzian Warehouse and Wholesale Shoe Store, 1895
Emerson Hadley House, 1895
J. J. Hill Seminary, 1892–99
Frederick Ingersoll House, 1889
Double House for William Lightner and George Young, 1886
*William Lightner House, 1893
Crawford Livingston House, 1898
Edgar C. Long House, 1889
Archibald MacLaren House, 1887
David McCourt House, 1887
Minnesota Club, 1892; addition, 1899 (demolished)
*Minnesota State Capitol, 1895–1905
*Charles P. Noyes House, 1887–89
Charles E. Riggs House, 1885
*St. Clement's Episcopal Church, 1894–95
George C. Squires House, 1889
*Virginia Street (Swedenborgian) Church, 1886
Albert P. Warren House, 1889

White Bear Lake
*A. Kirby Barnum Cottage, Dellwood, 1884
C. W. Bunn House, Manitou Island, 1895
William B. Dean Cottage, Manitou Island, 1893
Mrs. R. B. Galusha House, Cottage Grove, 1892
J. N. Granger House, 1890
*Walter S. Morton Cottage, c.1891
James H. Skinner House, Manitou Island, 1894
Lane K. Stone Cottage, 1892
*J. B. Tarbox Cottage, 1889–91

Willmar
*Great Northern Railroad Depot, 1891 (demolished)

MISSOURI
St. Louis
Louisiana Purchase Exposition, St. Louis, 1904
  *Festival Hall, 1904 (dismantled, 1905)
  *Palace of Fine Arts (Art Building), 1901–4, now St. Louis Art Museum; Richardson Memorial Library addition, 1914–15
St. Louis Public Library, 1907–12

MONTANA
Butte
State Savings Bank, 1906

Helena
Helena Hotel, 1912
Montana Club, 1906
St. Peter's Hospital and Brewer Pavilion, 1908

NEW JERSEY
Bayonne
Bayonne Bridge over Kill van Kull, 1928–31

Newark
*American Insurance Company Building, 1902–5; alterations, 1921–24 (demolished)
*Essex County Courthouse, 1901–2
Kinney Building, 1913–15; alterations, 1928
National State Savings Bank, 1912
Prudential Insurance Company Bridges and Buildings, 1926–29
Scheuer Building, 1905 (demolished)

Trenton
Trenton Industrial School, 1909–15

NEW YORK
New York City
American Academy of Arts and Letters, auditorium, 1928–30
*Austin, Nichols and Company Warehouse, Brooklyn, 1909–23
*Broadway Chambers Building, 1899–1900
*Federal Courthouse, Foley Square, 1929–36
*George Washington Bridge, over the Hudson River, 1926–31 (project not executed)
Interzone Building, 1922–23
*New York County Lawyer's Association, 1930
*New York Life Insurance Company Building, 1925–28
130 West Thirtieth Street Building (SJM Warehouse), 1926–27
R. C. Williams Warehouse, 1927–28
*Rodin Studio Apartment Building, 1916–17
*Union Club, 1901–3 (demolished)
*United States Custom House, 1899–1907
*United States Military Ocean Terminal (Army Supply Base), Brooklyn, 1918–19
*West Street Building, 1905–7
*F. W. Woolworth Company Building, 1910–13

Pelham Manor
*New York, New Haven and Hartford Railroad Depot, 1907

Port Morris
*New York, New Haven and Hartford Railroad Depot, 1907

OHIO
Cincinnati
*Union Central Life Insurance Company Building, 1911–13, now Central Trust Tower

Oberlin
*Allen Memorial Art Building, Oberlin College, 1914–17
Allen Memorial Hospital, 1924–25
Cox Administration Building, Oberlin College, 1914–15
*Finney Memorial Chapel, Oberlin College, 1905–8
Theological Group, Oberlin College, 1930–31

OREGON
Portland
Spalding Building, 1909

TEXAS
Austin
*Education Building (Sutton Hall), University of Texas, 1915–18
*Library (Battle Hall), University of Texas, 1909–11

WASHINGTON, D.C.
United States Chamber of Commerce, 1921–30
*United States Supreme Court Building, 1928–35
United States Treasury Department Annex, 1917–22

WEST VIRGINIA
Wheeling
West Virginia State Capitol and Main Building (with Cass Gilbert Jr.), 1924–32

WISCONSIN
Madison
Madison High School, 1905 (demolished)

New Richmond
O. W. Mosher House, 1893

READINGS

The following represents a selection of readily available secondary
sources on Cass Gilbert. Please consult the notes for primary materials.

Blodgett, Geoffrey. "Cass Gilbert, Architect: Conservative at Bay." *Journal of American History* 72 (December 1985): 615–36.

———. *Oberlin College Architecture: A Short History.* Oberlin, Ohio: Oberlin College, 1979.

———. "President King and Cass Gilbert: The Grand Collaboration." *Oberlin Alumni Magazine* 79 (winter 1983): 15–19.

Bluestone, Daniel. "Detroit's City Beautiful and the Problem of Commerce." *Journal of the Society of Architectural Historians* 47 (September 1988): 245–62.

Coles, William A. "The History of America's Greatest Fountain: The Scott Memorial Fountain on Belle Isle, Detroit." *Classical America* 3 (1973): 5–26.

Conforti, Michael, ed. *Minnesota 1900: Art and Life on the Upper Mississippi, 1890–1915.* Newark: University of Delaware Press, 1994.

Cornfeld, Richard. "The Poetic Vision: The Design of the St. Louis World's Fair." *Classical America* 3 (1973): 56–66.

Federman, Peter. "The Detroit Public Library." *Classical America* 4 (1977): 85–112.

Fenske, Gail, and Deryck Holdsworth. "Corporate Identity and the New York Office Building: 1895–1915." In *The Landscape of Modernity,* ed. Olivier Zunz, 129–59. New York: Russell Sage Foundation, 1992.

Gaskie, Margaret F. "The Woolworth Tower: A Technology Revisited." *Architectural Record,* mid-August 1981, 90–95.

Gordon, John Steele. "Woolworth's Cathedral." *American Heritage* 10 (July/August 1988): 16ff.

Greenberg, Allan, and Stephen Kieran. "The United States Supreme Court Building, Washington, D.C." *Antiques Magazine* (October 1985): 760–69.

Irish, Sharon. "A 'Machine that Makes the Land Pay': The West Street Building in New York." *Technology and Culture* 30 (April 1989): 376–97.

———. "West Hails East: Cass Gilbert in Minnesota." *Minnesota History* 53, no. 5 (spring 1993): 196–207.

Jones, Robert Allen. "Mr. Woolworth's Tower: The Skyscraper as Popular Icon." *Journal of Popular Culture* 7 (fall 1973): 408–24.

concrete-column-and-slab construction system, 148, 184n
Condit, Carl W., 180n, 185n
consumer culture, 132–33
Cook, Walter, 181n
Cox, Kenyon, 69
Cox Administration Building (Oberlin College, Ohio), 89
Cronin, John T., 124
Cushing, Luther Stearns, 50, 173n, 174n, 176n
Custom House, United States (New York, N.Y.). See United States Custom House

Daly, Raymond, 175n
Day, Frank Miles, 177n, 181n
Dayton Avenue Presbyterian Church (St. Paul, Minn.), 26, 29, 32, 87, 173n; 6; 15
Detroit Public Library (Mich.), 106, 108, 120, 181n; 83, 84
Dewey, George, 60
D. H. Burnham and Company, 120
Donnelly, John, 183n
Draper, Joan, 171n, 172n, 179n
Duchamp, Marcel, 12, 170n
DuFais, John, 68, 177n
Duluth Board of Trade (Minn.), 173n
Durham Cathedral (England), 134; 1, 18

Eames and Young, 181n
Eaton, Mrs. Theodore, 31
eclecticism, 20, 60, 134, 170n, 173n
Ecole des Beaux-Arts (Paris), 12, 14, 46, 61, 81
Education Building (now Sutton Hall; University of Texas, Austin), 103, 106; 82
Egbert, Donald Drew, 185n
Egyptian pyramids and obelisks, sketch of, 1
Emerson, Ralph Waldo, 164, 165
Emerson, William Ralph, 24–25, 173n
Endicott, Henry, 34, 50
Endicott, William, Jr., 34, 50
Endicott Building (St. Paul, Minn.), 34, 37, 50, 174n; 24, 25, 26
English cathedrals, 134, 136
Essex County Courthouse (Newark, N.J.), 69, 71, 76; 52, 53, 55
expositions, 74, 76, 81. See also specific expositions

Federal Courthouse (New York, N.Y.), 136; 107
Fenske, Gail, 175n, 183n
Festival Hall for Louisiana Purchase Exposition (St. Louis, Mo.), 76, 81, 84, 178n; 12; 60
Finch, Henry Martyn, 16
Fine Arts Building (Chicago, Ill.), 81, 179n
Finney, Frederick Norton, 179n
Finney Memorial Chapel (Oberlin College, Ohio), 86–87, 179n; 14, 15; 65

Flatiron Building (New York, N.Y.), 120; 91
Ford, Henry, 142
Ford Motor Company plant annex (Highland Park, Mich.), 142; 116
Foulds, William P., 64, 177n; 10
Foundation Company, 128
Foundling Hospital (Florence, Italy), 89
"Four Continents, The" (French), 68
French, Daniel Chester, 40, 68, 177n
Freynet, Jacques-Eugène, 46
Fuller Company, 50, 53, 54, 56–57, 175–76n
F. W. Woolworth Company Building (New York, N.Y.), 123, 128, 132–34, 136, 149, 151, 170n, 182–83n; 1, 23, 24; 93–105, 133

Garber and Woodward, 136
George A. Fuller Company, 50, 53, 54, 56–57, 175–76n
George Washington Bridge (New York, N.Y.), 155; 124
Georgian Revival style, 22, 155
German Bethlehem Presbyterian Church (St. Paul, Minn.), 30, 173n; 17, 18
Gilbert, Cass
  Anglophilia of, 97, 155, 183–84n, 185n
  birth of, 14
  coherence of design, 162, 165
  consistency in work, 58, 60, 162, 165
  education of, 13, 14
  enters McKim, Mead and White, 13, 15
  European travels of, 14–15, 19, 38
  expansion of practice, 50
  hiring practices, 97
  honorary awards and degrees, 180–81n
  move to New York City, 46, 50–71
  national leadership in civic design, 74–109
  on ornament, 148–49
  partnership with Taylor, 16–32, 171n
  professional organizations, 97, 180–81n
  on self-reliance, 164
  solo practice, 31–32, 34, 185n
  stylistic choices of, 13, 58, 60, 155, 157
  training by, 46
  watercolor sketchbooks, 14–15, 19
Gilbert, Cass, Jr. (son), 172n, 179n
Gilbert, Charles Champion (grandfather), 171n
Gilbert, Elizabeth Fulton Wheeler (mother), 14, 172n
  house (St. Paul, Minn.), 19, 21; 4
Gilbert, Julia Finch (wife), 16, 60, 172n
Gilbert, Mahlon, 173n
Gilbert, Samuel Augustus (father), 14, 172n
Gilbert and Taylor (firm), 16, 18–32, 34, 46; 6, 7; 1, 3, 4, 8, 10, 12, 15, 16, 17, 18, 24, 25, 26
Girault, Charles, 178n

Glessner, J. J., house (Chicago, Ill.), 22; 7
Godefroy, Jules-Alexis, 46
Gothic Revival style, 31, 114, 123, 128, 151
Gotzian, Paul, house (St. Paul, Minn.), 19, 21; 1
Gotzian Warehouse and Wholesale Shoe Store (St. Paul, Minn.), 19–20; 2
Great Exhibition (London; 1851), 74
Great Northern Railroad, 18, 32, 34
  Anoka depot (Minn.), 32, 173n; 22
  Little Falls depot (Minn.), 34
  Willmar depot (Minn.), 32, 173n; 23
grillage foundation, 176n, 177n
Grossman, Elizabeth, 106, 182n
Guastavino, Rafael, 65, 66, 84
Guérin, Jules, 12
Gunvald Aus and Co., 128, 184n

Harrison, Burt Sylvanus, 174n
Haskell, Samuel-Stevens, 46, 61, 68, 69, 174n, 176n, 177n
Hastings, Thomas, 61, 178n. See also Carrère and Hastings
Havemeyer Building (New York, N.Y.), 54
Haviland, John, 178n
Hay house (Washington, D.C.), 173n
Hébrard, Ernest-Michel, 61, 68
Hemenway house (Manchester-by-the-Sea, Mass.), 24–25; 9
Henderson, Lightner, 58, 176n
Henry C. Turner Construction Company, 148, 184n
Herter Brothers, 15
Hiedeman, Neil, 173n
Hill, James J., 18, 172n
Hoadley, David, 180n
Hogan, Edward J., 123
Holtzman, Stephen F., 128, 184n
Holyoke, Thomas, 46, 54; 8
Horowitz, Louis, 123
houses. See also specific houses
  city, 18–19, 20–22
  summer, 22, 24–26
Howe, Frank, 76
Howe, Jeffrey, 170n
Hudson and River Falls Railroad, 14
Huxtable, Ada Louise, 67

Institute of Arts and Letters, 97
Irving National Bank, 123, 128
Ittner, William B., 181n
Ives, Halsey Cooley, 81, 84, 179n
Ives Memorial Library (New Haven, Conn.), 95, 103, 155, 180n; 71

Jefferson, Thomas, 185n
Johnson, Thomas R., 64, 68, 81, 123, 177n; 11, 23, 24, 25; 51, 95, 97, 133
Johnston, Clarence H., 14, 15, 30, 31, 32, 171n

Kahn, Albert, 142, 184n
Kahn, Julius, 142
Kahn, Moritz, 142

Keally, G. S., **21**
Keeler, Timothy, 97
Keeler Tavern (Ridgefield, Conn.), 97, 180*n*
Kent, William, house (Tuxedo Park, N.Y.), 25–26; *11*
Kihlstedt, Folke Tyko, 178*n*
Kimball, Thomas R., 177*n*
King, Henry Churchill, 179*n*

Labrouste, Henri, 100
Labrouste, Théodore, 185*n*
Laloux, Victor, 46
Landau, Sarah Bradford, 175*n*
Latin Quarter (Paris), watercolors of, **2, 3**
Laurentian Library (Florence), 103
Le Corbusier, 12, 170*n*, 184*n*
Lee, Antoinette, 171*n*, 172*n*
Létang, Eugène, 13, 14, 71, 171*n*
libraries, 97, 100–103, 106, 108, 181*n*.
  See also specific libraries
Library of Congress building (Washington, D.C.), 67, 133, 183*n*
Lightner, William, house (St. Paul, Minn.), 22; **5;** *6*
Link, Theodore, 181*n*
Lockman, DeWitt McClellan, 14
Long, Birch Burdette, **19, 22**
Louisiana Purchase Exposition (St. Louis, Mo.; 1904), 74, 76, 81, 84, 178*n;* *57*
Louisiana Purchase Exposition Company, 74, 76, 178*n*, 179*n*
lych gate, 173*n*

Madison Square Garden (New York, N.Y.), 151, 185*n*
Marchand, John Omer, 46
Marshall, Henry Rutgers, 164
Masqueray, Emmanuel, **76,** 178*n*
Massachusetts Institute of Technology (M.I.T.), 13, 14, 46
Massachusetts State House (Boston), 53
Matters, Marion, 173*n*
Mauran, Russell and Garden, 181*n*
Mausolus, tomb of (Halicarnassus), 136
McKim, Mead and White, 13, 15, 16, 19, 21–22, 26, 34, 37, 38, 40, 71, 97, 100, 106, 151, 171*n*, 174*n*, 180*n*
McKinley, William, 61
mechanical engineering, 58
Mediterranean Revival style, 53, 84, 89, 103, 106, 181*n*
Metropolitan Life Tower (New York, N.Y.), 128
Michelangelo Buonarroti, 103
Military Ocean Terminal, United States (Brooklyn, N.Y.). *See* United States Military Ocean Terminal
Millet, Frank, 69
Minneapolis, Minnesota, 14, 16
Minnesota Club (St. Paul), 18, 172*n*
Minnesota State Capitol (St. Paul), 38, 40, 44, 46, 174*n;* **1, 26;** *28, 29, 32–36*
models, use of, 67

Monreale (Sicily), interior of cloister, watercolor of, **17**
monuments, sketch of world, **1**
Morton, Walter S., cottage (White Bear Lake, Minn.), 25; *10*
Municipal Building (Waterbury, Conn.), 155, 185*n;* *125, 126, 127*
Murphy, Patricia, 22, 26, 173*n*

National Academy of Design, 97
Neutra, Richard, 12, 170*n*, 184*n*
Newark, New Jersey, 69, 71
Newcomb, Victor, house (Elberon, N.J.), 26; *13*
New Haven Civic Improvement Committee (Conn.), 95, 96
New York Bar Association, 155, 157
New York County Lawyer's Association (N.Y.), 155, 157; *128*
New York Life Insurance Company Building (N.Y.), 151, 153; *119–23*
New York, New Haven and Hartford Railroad, 95–97, 180*n*
  Hunts Point Depot (N.Y.), 97
  New Haven Depot (Conn.), 95–96, 180*n;* *72*
  Pelham Manor Depot (N.Y.), 96–97; *74*
  Port Morris Depot (N.Y.), 96; *73*
New York Public Library (N.Y.), 61, 97, 100, 181*n*
Norris Estate Building (Boston, Mass.). *See* Brazer Building
North Congregational Church (Springfield, Mass.), 29
Northern Pacific Beneficial Association Hospital (Brainerd, Minn.), 171*n*
Northern Pacific Railroad, 15
Notre Dame Cathedral (Paris), sketch of, **1**
Noyes, Charles P., house (St. Paul, Minn.), 21–22; *4*

Oberlin College (Ohio), 86–87, 89, 179–80*n*
O'Connor, Andrew, 69, 178*n*
office buildings. *See* tall office buildings *and specific buildings by name*
Ohio Society of New York, 180*n*
Olmsted, Frederick Law, Jr., 95, 96
Otis Elevators, 148
Overby, Osmund, 179*n*

Palace of Fine Arts (Art Building; later St. Louis Art Museum) (St. Louis, Mo.), 76, 81, 84, 106, 178–79*n;* **1;** *56, 58, 59, 61, 62, 63*
Palmer and Hornbostel, 181*n*
Paris, Francklyn, 120
Paris and Wiley, 118, 120
Paris Exhibition (1889), 74, 76, 178*n*
Parthenon (Athens), sketch of, **1**
Peabody and Stearns, 20
Peabody, Stearns and Furber, 18
Peirce, John, Company, 66–67, 177*n*
Perth Amboy Terra Cotta Company, 176*n*
Petit Palais (Paris), 178*n*

Phillips, E. S. J., 164
Pierson, Louis, 123
piles, 114
Pioneer Building (St. Paul, Minn.), 34
Platt, Thomas "Boss," 61
polychrome terra cotta. *See* terra cotta
Porter, Alexander S., 50, 54, 174*n*
Portland Terrace (St. Paul, Minn.), 20; *3*
Post, George B., 54
Presbyterian Church, 16
Price, Bruce, 25–26, 54
Purdy, Corydon, 58, 176*n*
Pyle, Howard, 69

quadriga (St. Paul, Minn.), 40

Rachac, John R., Jr., 46, 81, 96, 185*n;* *22, 23*
racial typecasting, 133, 183*n*
Radcliffe, Abraham M., 14, 171*n*
railroad depots, 32, 34, 95–97. *See also specific depots*
real-estate development, 34, 50, 53, 56–58, 118, 123, 128
reinforced concrete, 89, 142, 148
Renaissance Revival style, 21, 34, 37–38, 40, 103, 108
Rhode Island State Capitol (Providence), 38, 40, *30, 31*
Ricci, Eliseo, 183*n*
Richardson, Henry Hobson, 21, 22, 26, 29, 173*n*
Ritter, Louis, 174*n*
Rockart (née Rachac), John R., Jr. *See* John R. Rachac Jr.
Rockcastle, Garth, 183*n*
Rodin Studio Apartment Building (New York, N.Y.), 89, 95; *70*
Romanesque Revival style, 21, 114
Root, John, 16, 173*n*
Ross, Albert R., 181*n*
Russell and Erwin Building (RussWin Hotel) (New Britain, Conn.), 37, 174*n;* *27*
RussWin Hotel (New Britain, Conn.). *See* Russell and Erwin Building

St. Clement's Church (New York, N.Y.), 31, 32
St. Clement's Episcopal Church (St. Paul, Minn.), 31–32, 173*n;* **7;** *19, 20*
St.-Gilles-du-Gard (France), 179*n*
St. James Building (New York, N.Y.), 54
St. John the Divine Episcopal Church (Moorhead, Minn.), 32; *21*
St. Louis Art Museum (Mo.). *See* Palace of Fine Arts
St. Louis Public Library (Mo.), 84, 100–103, 108, 181*n;* **19;** *76, 77, 78*
San Marco (Venice, Italy), sketch of, **1**
St. Paul, Minnesota, 14, 16, 18–46, 172*n*
St. Peter's (Rome), 38
St. Thomas Episcopal Church (New York, N.Y.), **1**
Sawyer, Philip, 181*n*
Schuyler, Montgomery, 29

194

Scott, James, Memorial Fountain
(Detroit, Mich.), 108–9, 182n; **21;**
85
Scottish Provident Institute, 176n
Seymour, George Dudley, 95
Shaw, Richard Norman, 31
Shingle Style, 19, 22, 26
Sibley, Henry H., 172n
skyline, 134
skyscrapers. *See* tall office buildings *and
specific buildings by name*
Smithmeyer and Pelz, 133
Society of the Cincinnati, 97
Sons of the American Revolution, 180n,
183n
Southack, Frederick, 56–57
Speck, Lawrence W., 181n
Spiers, Edward, 16
Squires, George, 18, 172n
Starin, John, 118, 182n
Starin Transportation Company, 118
Starrett, Theodore, 56, 57, 58, 176n
Starrett, William Aiken, 184n
Steedman Architectural Library (St.
Louis, Mo.), 181n
Stewart, A. T., department store (New
York, N.Y.), 54
Street, George Edmund, 31
Sullivan, Louis, 12, 13, 114
Supreme Court Building, United
States (Washington, D.C.). *See*
United States Supreme Court
Building
Sutton Hall (formerly Education Build-
ing; University of Texas, Austin),
103, 106; *82*
Swedenborg, Emmanuel, 173n
Swedenborgian Virginia Street Church
(St. Paul, Minn.), 26, 29–30, 32,
173n; *16*

Taj Mahal (Agra, India), sketch of, **1**
Talbot, Arthur Newell, 184n
Tallmadge, Thomas, 20
tall office buildings, 50, 53, 60, 114, 120,
123, 149, 151, 172n, 175n, 182n,
183n. *See also specific buildings by
name*
150-story fantasy office building, *92*
requirements of, 114
Tarbox, J. B., cottage (White Bear Lake,
Minn.), 26; *12, 14*
Taylor, H. A. C., house (Newport, R.I.),
21–22; *5*
Taylor, H. Knox, 16, 18
Taylor, Isaac S., 76, 178n
Taylor, James Knox, 14, 16, 25–26, 32,
61, 171n, 172n, 177n. *See also*
Gilbert and Taylor
terra cotta, 53, 54, 58, 89, 95, 106, 128,
136, 175n, 176n, 183n
Thompson, William H., 76
Thompson-Starrett Company, 123, 176n
Town and Country Club (St. Paul,
Minn.), 18
toxement, 184n
Trans-Mississippi Exposition (Omaha,
Neb.; 1898), 178n

Trinity Church Rectory (Boston, Mass.),
173n
Tunick, Susan, 176n
Turner, Claude Allen Porter, 148
Turner Construction Company, 148,
184n

Union Central Life Insurance Company
Building (now Central Trust
Tower) (Cincinnati, Oh.), 136; *106*
Union Club (New York, N.Y.), 68, 71,
177n; *50, 51*
Union Station (New Haven, Conn.),
95–96, 180n; *72*
United States Coast and Geodetic
Survey, 14
United States Coast Survey, 14
United States Custom House (New
York, N.Y.), 50, 60–61, 64–68, 71,
133, 170n, 176n, 177n, 183n; **1, 10,
11;** *44–49*
United States Military Ocean Terminal
(Brooklyn, N.Y.), 46, 136, 142,
148–49, 170n, 184n; *110–15, 117,
118*
United States Supreme Court Building
(Washington, D.C.), 40, 120, 157,
162, 185n; *129–32*
Universal Exposition (Paris; 1900), 78,
178n
University of Minnesota (Minneapolis),
86, 179n
University of Texas (Austin), 103, 106,
181n; *79*
University of Texas Library (now Battle
Hall; Austin), 103, 106; **20;** *80, 81*

Van Zanten, David, 181n
Villard, Henry, 15, 16, 171n
Villard houses (New York, N.Y.), 37,
174n
Viollet-le-Duc, 171n
Virginia Street Church (St. Paul,
Minn.), 26, 29–30, 32, 173n; *16*
Von Klenze, Leo, 185n

Wainwright Building (St. Louis, Mo.),
114
Walker, C. Howard, 76, 178n
Ware, William Robert, 14, 60
warehouses, 34, 136, 148. *See also specific
buildings by name*
Washington University (St. Louis, Mo.),
68, 76
Waterbury Club (Waterbury, Conn.),
155; *127*
Wells, George, 67, 68, 69, 178n
Wells, Joseph Morrill, 37, 174n
West Street Building (New York, N.Y.),
67, 114, 118, 120, 123, 134, 182n;
22; *86–91*
White, R. H., Warehouse Store
(Boston), 20
White, Stanford, 179n
Whitney, William Channing, 178n
Wilby, Ernest, 142
Willett, Arthur B., 87
Wilson, Woodrow, 128

Winans, Ross, house (Baltimore, Md.),
15
Winslow House (St. Paul, Minn.), 171n
Woolworth, Frank Winfield, 123, 128,
132, 182n
Woolworth Company Building (New
York, N.Y.). *See* F. W. Woolworth
Company Building
world monuments, sketch of, **1**
World's Columbian Exposition
(Chicago; 1893), 74, 81
World War I, 136
Wren, Christopher, 40
Wright, Frank Lloyd, 12, 13

Yamasaki, Leinweber and Associates,
180n

Zanesville, Ohio, 14